COUNTRY PROFILE: CHINA

COUNTRY

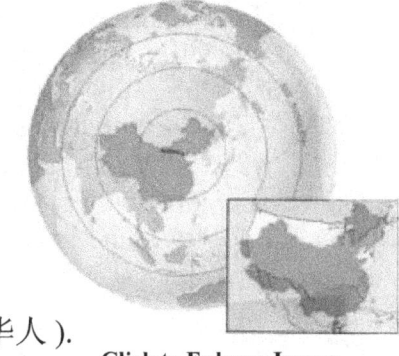

Click to Enlarge Image

Formal Name: People's Republic of China
(Zhonghua Renmin Gonghe Guo — 中华人民共和国).

Short Form: China (Zhongguo — 中国).

Term for Citizen(s) Chinese (singular and plural) (Huaren — 华人).

Capital: Beijing (Northern Capital — 北京).

Major Cities: Based on 2000 census data, the largest cities are the four centrally administered municipalities, which include dense urban areas, suburbs, and large rural areas: Chongqing (30.5 million), Shanghai (16.4 million), Beijing (13.5 million), and Tianjin (9.8 million). Other major cities are Wuhan (5.1 million), Shenyang (4.8 million), Guangzhou (3.8 million), Chengdu (3.2 million), Xi'an (3.1 million), and Changchun (3 million). China has 12 other cities with populations of between 2 million and 2.9 million and 20 or more other cities with populations of more than 1 million persons.

Independence: The outbreak of revolution on October 10, 1911, signaled the collapse of the Qing Dynasty (1644–1911), which was formally replaced by the government of the Republic of China on February 12, 1912. The People's Republic of China was officially established on October 1, 1949, replacing the Republic of China government on mainland China.

Public Holidays: The official national holidays are New Year's Day (January 1); Spring Festival or Lunar New Year (movable dates—three days—in January and February), Labor Day (May 1), and National Day (two-day observance on October 1–2). Also commemorated are International Women's Day (March 8), Youth Day (May 4), Children's Day (June 1), Chinese Communist Party Founding Day (July 1), Army Day (August 1), and Teachers' Day (September 10).

Flag: The flag of China is red with a large yellow five-pointed star and four smaller yellow five-pointed stars (arranged in a vertical arc toward the middle of the flag) in the upper hoist-side corner. The color red symbolizes the spirit of the revolution, and the five stars signify the unity of the people of China under the leadership of the Chinese Communist Party. The flag was officially unveiled in Beijing's Tiananmen Square on October 1, 1949, the formal announcement of the founding of the People's Republic of China.

Click to Enlarge Image

HISTORICAL BACKGROUND

Prehistory: Hominid activity dates back 4 to 5 million years in China, and evidence has been found of early paleolithic hominids living some 1 million years ago. The remains of *Homo erectus* (Peking Man or *Sinanthropus pekinensis*), found southwest of Beijing in 1927, date from around 400,000 years ago. Some 7,000 neolithic sites (some as old as ca. 9000 B.C.) have been found in North China, the Yangzi (Changjiang or Yangtze) River Valley, and southeast coastal areas. These sites include a neolithic agricultural village in Shaanxi Province dating from around 4500 B.C. to 3750 B.C., which had a moat for security and evidence of wood-framed, mud and straw houses, colored pottery, slash-and burn farming, and burial sites in nearby cemeteries. The oldest neolithic city found in China was uncovered by archaeologists in Henan Province and dates back to between 4,800 and 5,300 years ago.

Early History: The first recognized dynasty—the Xia—lasted from about 2200 to 1750 B.C. and marked the transition from the late neolithic age to the Bronze Age. The Xia was the beginning of a long period of cultural development and dynastic succession that led the way to the more urbanized civilization of the Shang Dynasty (1750–1040 B.C.). Hereditary Shang kings ruled over much of North China, and Shang armies fought frequent wars against neighboring settlements and nomadic herders from the north. The Shang capitals were centers of sophisticated court life for the king, who was the shamanistic head of the ancestor- and spirit-worship cult. Intellectual life developed in significant ways during the Shang period and flourished in the next dynasty—the Zhou (1040–256 B.C.). China's great schools of intellectual thought—Confucianism, Legalism, Daoism, Mohism, and others—all developed during the Zhou Dynasty.

The intersection of migration, amalgamation, and development has characterized China's history from its earliest origins and resulted in a distinctive system of writing, philosophy, art, and social and political organization and civilization that was continuous over the past 4,000 years. Since the beginning of recorded history (at least since the Shang Dynasty), the people of China have developed a strong sense of their origins, both mythological and real, and kept voluminous records concerning both. As a result of these records, augmented by numerous archaeological discoveries in the second half of the twentieth century, information concerning the ancient past, not only of China but also of much of East, Central, and Inner Asia, has survived.

The Imperial Period: Over several millennia, China absorbed the people of surrounding areas into its own civilization while adopting the more useful institutions and innovations of the conquered people. Peoples on China's peripheries were attracted by such achievements as its early and well-developed ideographic written language, technological developments, and social and political institutions. The refinement of the Chinese people's artistic talent and their intellectual creativity, plus the sheer weight of their numbers, has long made China's civilization predominant in East Asia. The process of assimilation continued over the centuries through conquest and colonization until the core territory of China was brought under unified rule. The Chinese polity was first consolidated and proclaimed an empire during the Qin Dynasty (221–206 B.C.). Although short-lived, the Qin Dynasty set in place lasting unifying structures, such as standardized legal codes, bureaucratic procedures, forms of writing, coinage, and a pattern of thought and scholarship. These were modified and improved upon by the successor Han Dynasty

(206 B.C.–A.D. 220). Under the Han, a combination of the stricter Legalism and the more benevolent, human-centered Confucianism—known as Han Confucianism or State Confucianism—became the ruling norm in Chinese culture for the next 2,000 years. Thus, the Chinese marked the cultures of people beyond their borders, especially those of Korea, Japan, and Vietnam.

Another recurrent historical theme has been the unceasing struggle of the largely agrarian Chinese against the threat posed to their safety and way of life by non-Chinese peoples on the margins of their territory. For centuries most of the foreigners that China's officials saw came from or through the Central and Inner Asian societies to the north and west. This circumstance conditioned the Chinese view of the outside world. The Chinese saw their domain as the self-sufficient center of the universe, and from this image they derived the traditional (and still used) Chinese name for their country—Zhongguo, literally Middle Kingdom or Central Nation. Those at the center (*zhong*) of civilization (as they knew it) distinguished themselves from the "barbarian" peoples on the outside (*wai*), whose cultures were presumed to be inferior by Chinese standards. For centuries, China faced periodic invasions from Central and Inner Asia—including major incursions in the twelfth century by the Khitan and the Jurchen, in the thirteenth century by the Mongols, and in the seventeenth century by the Manchu, all of whom left an imprint on Chinese civilization while heightening Chinese perceptions of threat from the north. Starting in the pre-Qin period, Chinese states built large defensive walls that, in time, composed a "Great Wall." The Great Wall is actually a series of noncontiguous walls, forts, and other defensive structures built or rebuilt during the Qin, Han, Sui (A.D. 589–618), Jin (1115–1234), and Ming (1368–1643) periods, rather than a single, continuous wall. The Great Wall reaches from the coast of Hebei Province to northwestern Gansu, officially 6,000 kilometers in length, although unofficial estimates range from 2,700 kilometers to as many as 50,000 kilometers, depending on which structures are included in the measurement.

The Tang (618–907) and Song (960–1279) dynasties represented high points of Chinese cultural development and interaction with distant foreign lands. The Yuan, or Mongol, Dynasty (1279–1368) was a period of foreign occupation but of even greater interaction with other cultures. Despite these periods of openness, which brought occasional Middle Eastern and European envoys and missionaries, the China-centered ("sinocentric") view of the world remained largely undisturbed until the nineteenth century when China first clashed with the European nations. The Manchu had conquered China and established the Qing Dynasty (1644–1911), ushering in a period of great conquest and a long period of relative peace. When Europeans began arriving in increasing numbers, Chinese courtiers expected them to conduct themselves according to traditional tributary relations that had evolved over the centuries between their emperor and representatives of Central Asian states who came via the Silk Road and others who came from Southeast Asia and the Middle East via the sea trade. The Western powers arrived in China in full force at a time of tremendous internal rebellion and rapid economic and social change. By the mid-nineteenth century, China had been defeated militarily by superior Western technology and weaponry, and the government was plagued with ever mounting rebellions. As it faced dynastic breakdown and imminent territorial dismemberment, China began to reassess its position with respect to its own internal development and the Western incursions. By 1911 the millennia-old dynastic system of imperial government was hastily toppled as a result of the efforts of a half century of reform, modernization, and, ultimately, revolution.

Republican China: The end of imperial rule was followed by nearly four decades of major socioeconomic development and sociopolitical discord. The initial establishment of a Western-style government—the Republic of China—was followed by several efforts to restore the throne. Lack of a strong central authority led to regional fragmentation, warlordism, and civil war. The main figure in the revolutionary movement that overthrew imperial rule was Sun Yatsen (1866–1925), who, along with other republican political leaders, endeavored to establish a parliamentary democracy. They were thwarted by warlords with imperial and quasi-democratic pretensions who resorted to assassination, rebellion, civil war, and collusion with foreign powers (especially Japan) in their efforts to gain control. A major political and social movement during this time was the May Fourth Movement (1919), in which calls for the study of "science" and "democracy" were combined with a new patriotism that became the focus of an anti-Japanese and antigovernment movement. Ignored by the Western powers and in charge of a southern military government with its capital in Guangzhou, Sun Yatsen eventually turned to the new Soviet Union for inspiration and assistance. The Soviets obliged Sun and his Guomindang (Nationalist Party). Soviet advisers helped the Guomindang establish political and military training activities. A key individual in these developments was Jiang Jieshi (1888–1975; Chiang Kai-shek in Yue dialect), one of Sun's lieutenants from the early revolution days. But Moscow also supported the new Chinese Communist Party (CCP), which was founded by Mao Zedong (1893–1976) and others in Shanghai in 1921. The Soviets hoped for consolidation of the Guomindang and the CCP but were prepared for either side to emerge victorious. The struggle for power in China began between the Guomindang and the CCP as both parties also sought the unification of China.

Sun's untimely death from illness in 1925 brought a split in the Guomindang and eventually an uneasy united front between the Guomindang and the CCP. Jiang Jieshi's military academy trained a new generation of officers who would soon embark on the Northern Expedition. Zhou Enlai (1898–1976), who later become premier of China under the communists, was a political commissar at this academy. Jiang, who succeeded Sun Yatsen, broke with his Soviet advisers and with the communists but by 1927 was successful in defeating the northern warlords and unifying China. The years 1928 to 1937 are often referred to as the Nanjing Decade because of the national development that took place under Jiang's presidency before World War II when China's capital was in Nanjing (Southern Capital). The Northern Expedition had culminated in the capture of Beijing, which was renamed Beiping (Northern Peace). Thereafter, the Nanjing government received international recognition as the sole legitimate government of China.

With the 1927 split between the Guomindang and the CCP, the CCP began to engage in armed struggle against the Jiang regime. The Red Army was established in 1927, and after a series of uprisings and internal political struggles, the CCP announced the establishment in 1931 of the Chinese Soviet Republic under the chairmanship of Mao in Jiangxi Province in south-central China. After a series of deadly annihilation campaigns by Jiang's armies, the Red Army and the CCP apparatus broke out of Jiangxi and embarked on their epic 12,500-kilometer Long March of 1934–35 to a new stronghold in Shaanxi Province in the north. During the march, Mao consolidated his hold over the CCP when in 1935 he became chairman, a position he held until his death in 1976.

4

Japan invaded Manchuria in 1931, established the puppet government of Manchukuo in 1932, and soon pushed south into North China. The 1936 Xi'an Incident—in which Jiang Jieshi was held captive by local military forces until he agreed to a second front with the CCP—brought new impetus to China's resistance to Japan. However, a clash between Chinese and Japanese troops outside Beiping on July 7, 1937, marked the beginning of full-scale warfare. Shanghai was attacked and quickly fell. An indication of the ferocity of Tokyo's determination to annihilate the Guomindang government is reflected in the major atrocity committed by the Japanese army in and around Nanjing during a six-week period in December 1937 and January 1938. Known in history as the Nanjing Massacre, wanton rape, looting, arson, and mass executions took place, so that in one horrific day, some 57,418 Chinese prisoners of war and civilians reportedly were killed. Japanese sources admit to a total of 142,000 deaths during the Nanjing Massacre, but Chinese sources report upward of 340,000 deaths and 20,000 women raped. Japan expanded its war effort in the Pacific, Southeast, and South Asia, and by 1941 the United States had entered the war. With Allied assistance, Chinese military forces—both Guomindang and CCP—defeated Japan. Civil war between the Guomindang and the CCP broke out in 1946, and the Guomindang forces were defeated and had retreated to a few offshore islands and Taiwan by 1949. Mao and the other CCP leaders reestablished the capital in Beiping, which they renamed Beijing.

People's Republic of China: The communist takeover of the mainland in 1949 set the scene for building a new society built on a Marxist-Leninist model replete with class struggle and proletarian politics fashioned and directed by the CCP. The People's Republic of China was barely established (October 1, 1949) when it perceived a threat from the United States, which was at war in North Korea, and elected to support its neighbor, the new communist state, the Democratic People's Republic of Korea. The Chinese People's Volunteer Army invaded the Korean Peninsula in October 1950 and, along with its North Korean ally, enjoyed initial military success and then a two-year stalemate, which culminated in an armistice signed on July 27, 1953. Meanwhile, China seized control of Tibet. It also had embarked on a political rectification movement against "enemies of the state" and promoting "class struggle" under the aegis of agrarian reform as part of the "transition to socialism."

Periods of consolidation and economic development facilitated by President Liu Shaoqi (1898–1969) and Premier Zhou were severely altered by disastrous anti-intellectual (such as the Hundred Flowers Campaign, 1957), economic (the Great Leap Forward, 1958–59), and political (the Great Proletarian Cultural Revolution, 1966–76) experiments directed by Mao and his supporters. During this time, China had broken with the Soviet Union by 1959, fought a border war with India in 1962, and skirmished with Soviet troops in 1969. In 1969 Mao anointed Lin Biao (1908–71), a radical People's Liberation Army marshal, as his heir apparent, but by 1971 Lin was dead, the result of an airplane crash in Mongolia following an alleged coup attempt against his mentor. Less radical leaders such as Zhou and Vice Premier Deng Xiaoping (1904–97), who had been politically rehabilitated after his disgrace early in the Cultural Revolution, asserted some control, and negotiations were initiated with the United States, ending a generation of extreme animosity toward Washington. The 1976 death of Mao ended the extremist influence in the party, and, under the leadership of Deng Xiaoping and his supporters, China began a period of pragmatic economic reforms and opening itself to the outside world.

Reform-era activities began in earnest in 1978 and eventually made China one of the largest world economies and trading partners as well as an emerging regional military power. The Four Modernizations (agriculture, industry, science and technology, and national defense) became the preeminent agenda within the party, state, and society. The well-being of China's people increased substantially, especially along coastal areas and in urban areas involved in manufacturing for the world market. Yet, politics, the so-called "fifth modernization," occurred at too slow a pace for the emerging generation. China's incipient democracy movement was subdued in 1978–79 at the very time that China's economic reforms were being launched. As Deng consolidated his control of China, the call for political reform came to the fore again in the mid-1980s, and pro-reform leaders were placed in positions of authority: Zhao Ziyang (1919–2005) was appointed premier, and Hu Yaobang (1915–89) CCP general secretary. Deng himself, satisfied with being the "power behind the throne," never held a top position. The democracy movement, however, was violently suppressed by the military in the 1989 Tiananmen incident.

In the years after Tiananmen, conservative reformers led by Deng protégé Jiang Zemin (later to become president of China, chairman of both the state Central Military Commission and party Central Military Commission, and general secretary of the CCP) endured and eventually overcame world criticism. When Deng went into retirement, the rising generation of technocrats ruled China and oversaw its modernization. Political progress gradually occurred. Term limits were placed on political and governmental positions at all levels, succession became orderly and contested elections began to take place at the local level. Tens of thousands of Chinese students went overseas to study; many returned to participate in the building of modern China, some to become millionaires in the new "socialist economy with Chinese characteristics." As a sign of its emerging superpower status, in October 2003 China launched its first "taikonaut" into space on a 22-hour journey. The second space launch, with two taikonauts, took place in October 2005 and involved a 115-hour flight. In the next stage of space exploration, China plans to conduct a space walk in 2007 and a rendezvous docking in orbit between 2009 and 2012. It also plans to launch a moon-orbiting unmanned spacecraft by 2007 and to land an unmanned probe on the moon by 2010.

As the twenty-first century began, a new generation of leaders emerged and gradually replaced the old. Position by position, Jiang Zemin gradually gave up his leadership role and by 2004 had moved into a position of elder statesman, still with obvious influence exerted through his protégés who were embedded at all levels of the government. The "politics in command" of the Maoist past were subliminally present when technocrat Hu Jintao emerged—by 2004—as the preeminent leader (president of China, chairman of both the state Central Military Commission and party Central Military Commission, and general secretary of the CCP) with grudging acceptance by Jiang and his supporters.

GEOGRAPHY

Location: Usually described as part of East Asia, China is south of Mongolia and the Siberian land mass, west of the Korean Peninsula and insular Japan, north of Southeast Asia, and east of Central and South Asia.

Click to Enlarge Image

Size: China has a total area of nearly 9,596,960 square kilometers. Included in this total are 9,326,410 square kilometers of land and 270,550 square kilometers of inland lakes and rivers. From east to west, the distance is about 5,000 kilometers from the Heilong Jiang (Amur River) to the Pamir Mountains in Central Asia; from north to south, the distance is approximately 4,050 kilometers from Heilongjiang Province to Hainan Province in the south and another 1,450 kilometers farther south to Zengmu Shoal, a territorial claim off the north coast of Malaysia.

Land Boundaries: China has a total of 22,117 kilometers of land boundaries with 14 other nations. These borders include: Afghanistan (76 kilometers), Bhutan (470 kilometers), Burma (2,185 kilometers), India (3,380 kilometers), Kazakhstan (1,533 kilometers), North Korea (1,416 kilometers), Kyrgyzstan (858 kilometers), Laos (423 kilometers), Mongolia (4,677 kilometers), Nepal (1,236 kilometers), Pakistan (523 kilometers), Russia (4,300 kilometers), Tajikistan (414 kilometers), and Vietnam (1,281 kilometers).

Length of Coastline: China's coastline extends 14,500 kilometers from the border with North Korea in the north to Vietnam in the south. China's coasts are on the East China Sea, Korea Bay, Yellow Sea, and South China Sea.

Maritime Claims: China claims a 12-nautical-mile territorial sea, a 24-nautical-mile contiguous zone, a 200-nautical-mile exclusive economic zone, and a 200-nautical-mile continental shelf or the distance to the edge of the continental shelf.

Boundary Disputes: China is involved in a complex dispute with Malaysia, Philippines, Taiwan, Vietnam, and possibly Brunei over the Spratly (Nansha) Islands in the South China Sea. The 2002 "Declaration on the Conduct of Parties in the South China Sea" eased tensions but fell short of a legally binding code of conduct desired by several of the disputants. China also occupies the Paracel (Xisha) Islands, which are also claimed by Vietnam and Taiwan, and asserts a claim to the Japanese-administered Senkaku Islands (Diaoyu Tai) in the Pacific Ocean. Most of the mountainous and militarized boundary with India is in dispute, but Beijing and New Delhi have committed to begin resolution with discussions on the least disputed middle sector. China's de facto administration of the Aksai Chin section of Kashmir (which is disputed by India and Pakistan) is the subject of a dispute between China and India. India does not recognize Pakistan's ceding lands to China in a 1964 boundary agreement. In October 2004, China signed an agreement with Russia on the delimitation of their entire 4,300-kilometer-long border, which had long been in dispute.

Topography: Mountains cover 33 percent of China's landmass, plateaus 26 percent, basins 19 percent, plains 12 percent, and hills 10 percent. Thus, 69 percent of China's land is mountains, hills, and highlands. China has five main mountain ranges, and seven of its mountain peaks are higher than 8,000 meters above sea level. The main topographic features include the Qingzang (Qinghai-Tibet) Plateau at 4,000 meters above sea level and the Kunlun, Qin Ling, and Greater Hinggan ranges. In the Himalaya Mountains, the world's highest, are Mount Everest (known in China as Qomolangma) at 8,844.4 meters (based on new official measurements) and K–2 at 8,611 meters, shared with Nepal and Pakistan, respectively. The lowest inland point in China—the second lowest place in the world after the Dead Sea—is at Turpan Pendi, 140 kilometers southeast of Urumqi, the capital of Xinjiang Uygur Autonomous Region, at 154 meters below sea level. With temperatures that have reached 49.6 C, it also ranks as one the hottest places in China.

Principal Rivers: China has 50,000 rivers totaling some 420,000 kilometers in length and each having a catchment area of more than 100 square kilometers. Some 1,500 of these rivers each have catchment areas exceeding 1,000 square kilometers. Most rivers flow from west to east and empty into the Pacific Ocean. The Yangzi (Changjiang or Yangzte River), which rises in Tibet, flows through Central China, and, having traveled 6,300 kilometers, enters the Yellow Sea near Shanghai. The Yangzi has a catchment area of 1.8 million square kilometers and is the third longest river in the world after the Amazon and the Nile. The second longest river in China is the Huanghe (Yellow River), which also rises in Tibet and travels circuitously for 5,464 kilometers through North China before reaching the Bo Hai Gulf on the north coast of Shangdong Province. It has a catchment area of 752,000 square kilometers. The Heilongjiang (Heilong or Black Dragon River) flows for 3,101 kilometers in Northeast China and an additional 1,249 in Russia, where it is known as the Amur. The longest river in South China is the Zhujiang (Pearl River), which is 2,214 kilometers long. Along with its three tributaries, the Xi, Dong, and Bei—West, East, and North—rivers, it forms the rich Zhujiang Delta near Guangzhou, Zhuhai, Macau, and Hong Kong. Other major rivers are the Liaohe in the northeast, Haihe in the north, Qiantang in the east, and Lancang in the southwest.

Climate: Most of the country is in the northern temperate zone. There are complex climatic patterns ranging from the cold-temperate north to the tropical south, with subarctic-like temperatures in the Himalaya Mountains, resulting in a temperature difference of some 40° C from north to south. Temperatures range from –30° C in the north in January to 28° C in the south in July. Annual precipitation varies significantly from region to region, with a high of 1,500 millimeters annually along the southeastern coast and a low of fewer than 50 millimeters in the northwest. There is an alternating wet monsoon in the summer and a dry monsoon in winter. North China and southward are affected by the seasonal cold, dry winds from Siberia and the Mongolia Plateau between September/October and March/April. Summer monsoon winds bring warm and wet currents into South China and northward.

Natural Resources: China has substantial mineral reserves and is the world's largest producer of antimony, natural graphite, tungsten, and zinc. Other major minerals are bauxite, coal, crude petroleum, diamonds, gold, iron ore, lead, magnetite, manganese, mercury, molybdenum, natural gas, phosphate rock, tin, uranium, and vanadium. With its vast mountain ranges, China's hydropower potential is the largest in the world.

Land Use: Based on 2005 estimates, 14.86 percent (about 1.4 million square kilometers) of China's land is arable. About 1.3 percent (some 116,580 square kilometers) is planted to permanent crops. With comparatively little land planted to permanent crops, intensive agricultural techniques are used to reap harvests that are sufficient to feed the world's largest population and still have surplus for export. An estimated 544,784 square kilometers of land were irrigated in 2004.

Environmental Factors: The major current environmental issues in China are air pollution (greenhouse gases and sulfur dioxide particulates) from overreliance on coal, which produces acid rain; water shortages, particularly in the north; water pollution from untreated wastes; deforestation; an estimated loss of 20 percent of agricultural land since 1949 to soil erosion and economic development; desertification; and illegal trade in endangered species. Deforestation has been a major contributor to China's most significant natural disaster: flooding. In 1998 some 3,656 people died and 230 million people were affected by flooding. China's national carbon dioxide (CO_2) emissions are among the highest in the world and increasing annually. The CO_2 emissions in 1991 were estimated at 2.4 billion tons; by 2000 that level, according to United Nations (UN) statistics, had increased by 16 percent to nearly 2.8 billion tons. According to the International Energy Agency (IEA), between 1990 and 2002 the increase was closer to 45 percent. These amounts cited by the UN are more than double those of India and Japan but still less than half those of the United States (comparable figures for Russia are unavailable but estimated at probably half the level of China's). China's ozone depleting potential also is high but was decreasing in the early twenty-first century. The CO_2 emissions are mostly produced by coal-burning energy plants and other coal-burning operations. Better pollution control and billion-dollar cleanup programs have helped reduced the growth rate of industrial pollution.

Time Zone: Although China crosses all or part of five international time zones, it operates on a single uniform time, China Standard Time (CST; Greenwich Mean Time plus eight hours), using Beijing as the base. China does not employ a daylight savings time system.

SOCIETY

Population: China officially recognized the birth of its 1.3 billionth citizen (not counting Hong Kong, Macau, or Taiwan) on January 5, 2005. U.S. Government sources put the population at an estimated 1,313,973,713 in July 2006. The annual population growth rate was estimated at 0.59 percent (2006 estimate).The nation's overall population density was 135 persons per square kilometer in 2003. The most densely populated provinces are in the east: Jiangsu (712 persons per square kilometer), Shangdong (587 persons per square kilometer), and Henan (546 persons per square kilometer). Shanghai was the most densely populated municipality at 2,646 persons per square kilometer. The least densely populated areas are in the west, with Tibet having the lowest density at only 2 persons per square kilometer. Sixty-two percent of the population lived in rural areas in 2004, while 38 percent lived in urban settings. About 94 percent of population lives on approximately 46 percent of land. Based on 2000 census data, the provinces with the largest populations were Henan (91.2 million), Shandong (89.9 million), Sichuan (82.3 million, not including Chongqing municipality, which was formerly part of Sichuan Province), and Guangdong (85.2 million). The smallest were Qinghai (4.8 million) and Tibet (2.6 million). In the long term, China faces increasing urbanization; according to predictions, nearly 70 percent of the population will live in urban areas by 2035.

Demography: China has been the world's most populous nation for many centuries. When China took its first post-1949 census in 1953, the population stood at 582 million; by the fifth census in 2000, the population had almost doubled, reaching 1.2 billion. China's fast-growing population was a major policy matter for its leaders in the mid-twentieth century, so that in the early 1970s, the government implemented a stringent one-child birth-control policy. As a result of that policy, China successfully achieved its goal of a more stable and much-reduced fertility rate; in 1971 women had an average of 5.4 children versus an estimated 1.7 children in 2004. Nevertheless, the population continues to grow, and people want more children. There is also a serious gender imbalance. Census data obtained in 2000 revealed that 119 boys were born for every 100 girls, and among China's "floating population" (*see* Migration below) the ratio was as high as 128:100. These situations led Beijing in July 2004 to ban selective abortions of female fetuses. Additionally, life expectancy has soared, and China now has an increasingly aging population; it is projected that 11.8 percent of the population in 2020 will be 65 years of age and older. Based on 2006 estimates, China's age structure is 0–14 years of age—20.8 percent; 15–64 years—71.4 percent, and 65 years and older—7.7 percent. Estimates made in 2006 indicate a birthrate of nearly 13.3 births per 1,000 and a death rate of 6.9 per 1,000. In 2006 life expectancy at birth was estimated at 74.5 years for women and 70.9 for men, or 72.6 years overall. The infant mortality rate was estimated at 23.1 per 1,000 live births overall (25.9 per 1,000 for females and 20.6 for males).

Migration: In 2006 it was estimated that China was experiencing a –0.39 per 1,000 population net migration rate. Of major concern in China is its growing "floating population" (*liudong renkou*), a large number of people moving from the countryside to the city, from developed economic areas to underdeveloped areas, and from the central and western regions to the eastern coastal region, as a result of fast-paced reform-era economic development and modern agricultural practices that have reduced the need for a large agricultural labor force. Although residency requirements have been relaxed to a degree, the floating population is not officially permitted to reside permanently in the receiving towns and cities. As early as 1994, it was estimated that China had a surplus of approximately 200 million agricultural workers, and the number was expected to increase to 300 million in the early twenty-first century and to expand even further into the long-term future. It was reported in 2005 that the floating population had increased from 70 million in 1993 to 140 million in 2003, thus exceeding 10 percent of the national population and accounting for 30 percent of all rural laborers. According to the 2000 national census, population flow inside a province accounted for 65 percent of the total while that crossing provincial boundaries accounted for 35 percent. Young and middle-aged people account for the vast majority of this floating population; those between 15 and 35 years of age account for more than 70 percent.

Other migration issues include the more than 2,000 Tibetans who cross into Nepal annually, according to the United Nations High Commissioner for Refugees (UNHCR). The government tries to prevent this out-migration from occurring and has pressured Nepalese authorities to repatriate illegal border-crossing Tibetans. Another activity viewed as illegal is the influx of North Koreans into northeastern China. Some 1,850 North Koreans fled their country in 2004, but China views them as illegal economic migrants rather than refugees and sends many of them back. Some of those who succeed in reaching sanctuary in foreign diplomatic compounds or international schools have been allowed to depart for South Korea.

Ethnic Groups: Besides the majority Han Chinese, China recognizes 55 other nationality or ethnic groups, numbering about 105 million persons, mostly concentrated in the northwest, north, northeast, south, and southwest but with some in central interior areas. Based on the 2000 census, some 91.5 percent of the population was classified as Han Chinese (1.1 billion). The other major minority ethnic groups were Zhuang (16.1 million), Manchu (10.6 million), Hui (9.8

million), Miao (8.9 million), Uygur (8.3 million), Tujia (8 million), Yi (7.7 million), Mongol (5.8 million), Tibetan (5.4 million), Bouyei (2.9 million), Dong (2.9 million), Yao (2.6 million), Korean (1.9 million), Bai (1.8 million), Hani (1.4 million), Kazakh (1.2 million), Li (1.2 million), and Dai (1.1 million). Classifications are often based on self-identification, and it is sometimes and in some locations advantageous for political or economic reasons to identify with one group over another. All nationalities in China are equal according to the law. Official sources maintain that the state protects their lawful rights and interests and promotes equality, unity, and mutual help among them.

Languages: The official language of China is standard Chinese or Mandarin (Putonghua, which means standard speech, based on the Beijing dialect). Other major dialects are Yue (Cantonese), Wu (Shanghaiese), Minbei (Fuzhou), Minnan (Hokkien-Taiwanese), Xiang, Gan, and Hakka (Kejia). Because of the many ethnic groups in China, numerous minority languages also are spoken.

All of the Chinese dialects share a common written form that has evolved and been standardized during two millennia and serves as a unifying bond amongst the Han Chinese. The government has aggressively developed both shorthand Chinese and Pinyin (phonetic spelling) as ways to increase literacy and transliterate Chinese names. The Pinyin system was introduced in 1958 and was approved by the State Council in 1978 as the standard system for the romanization of Chinese personal and geographic names. In 2000 the Hanyu (Han language) Pinyin phonetic alphabet was written into law as the unified standard for spelling and phonetic notation of the national language.

Religion: The traditional religions of China are Confucianism, Daoism, and Buddhism. Confucianism is not a religion, although some have tried to imbue it with rituals and religious qualities, but rather a philosophy and system of ethical conduct that since the fifth century B.C. has guided China's society. Kong Fuzi (Confucius in Latinized form) is honored in China as a great sage of antiquity whose writings promoted peace and harmony and good morals in family life and society in general. Ritualized reverence for one's ancestors, sometimes referred to as ancestor worship, has been a tradition in China since at least the Shang Dynasty (1750–1040 B.C.).

Estimates of the number of adherents to various beliefs are difficult to establish; as a percentage of the population, institutionalized religions, such as Christianity and Islam, represent only about 4 percent and 2 percent of the population, respectively. In 2005 the Chinese government acknowledged that there were an estimated 100 million adherents to various sects of Buddhism and some 9,500 and 16,000 temples and monasteries, many maintained as cultural landmarks and tourist attractions. The Buddhist Association of China was established in 1953 to oversee officially sanctioned Buddhist activities. In 1998 there reportedly were 600 Daoist temples and an unknown number of adherents in China. According to the U.S. Department of State in 2005, approximately 8 percent of the population is Buddhist, approximately 1.5 percent is Muslim, an estimated 0.4 percent belongs to the government-sponsored "patriotic" Catholic Church, an estimated 0.4 to 0.6 percent belongs to the unofficial Vatican-affiliated Roman Catholic Church, and an estimated 1.2 to 1.5 percent is registered as Protestant. However, both Protestants and Catholics also have large underground communities, possibly numbering as many as 90 million.

Chinese government figures from 2004 estimate 20 million adherents of Islam in China, but unofficial estimates suggest a much higher total. Most adherents of Islam are members of the Uygur and Hui nationality people.

The Falun Dafa (Wheel of Law, also called Falun Gong) quasi-religious movement based on traditional Chinese *qigong* (deep-breathing exercises) and Daoist and Buddhist practices and beliefs was established in 1992 and claimed 70 million to 100 million practitioners in China in the late 1990s. Because of its perceived antigovernment activities, Falun Gong was outlawed in China in April 1999, and reportedly tens of thousands of its practitioners were arrested and sentenced to "reeducation through labor" or incarcerated in mental hospitals. The constitution grants citizens of the People's Republic of China the freedom of religious belief and maintains that the state "protects normal religious activities," but that no one "may make use of religion to engage in activities that disrupt public order, impair the health of citizens or interfere with the educational system of the state."

Education and Literacy: Education in China is the responsibility of the Ministry of Education. The population has had on average only 6.2 years of schooling, but in 1986 the goal of nine years of compulsory education by 2000 was established. The education system provides free primary education for five years, starting at age seven, followed by five years of secondary education for ages 12 to 17. At this level, there are three years of middle school and two years of high school. The Ministry of Education reports a 99 percent attendance rate for primary school and an 80 percent rate for both primary and middle schools. Since free higher education was abolished in 1985, applicants to colleges and universities compete for scholarships based on academic ability. Private schools have been allowed since the early 1980s.

The United Nations Development Programme reported that in 2003 China had 116,390 kindergartens with 613,000 teachers and 20 million students. At that time, there were 425,846 primary schools with 5.7 million teachers and 116.8 million students. General secondary education had 79,490 institutions, 4.5 million teachers, and 85.8 million students. There also were 3,065 specialized secondary schools with 199,000 teachers and 5 million students. Among these specialized institutions were 6,843 agricultural and vocational schools with 289,000 teachers and 5.2 million students and 1,551 special schools with 30,000 teachers and 365,000 students. In 2003 China supported 1,552 institutions of higher learning (colleges and universities) and their 725,000 professors and 11 million students. While there is intense competition for admission to China's colleges and universities among college entrants, Beijing and Qinghua universities and more than 100 other key universities are the most sought after. The literacy rate in China is 90.9 percent, based on 2002 estimates.

Health: Indicators of the status of China's health sector can be found in the nation's fertility rate of 1.8 children per woman (a 2005 estimate) and an under-five-years-of-age mortality rate of 37 per 1,000 live births (a 2003 estimate). In 2002 China had nearly 1.7 physicians per 1,000 persons and about 2.4 beds per 1,000 persons in 2000. Health expenditures on a purchasing parity power (PPP) basis were US$224 per capita in 2001, or 5.5 percent of gross domestic product (GDP). Some 37.2 percent of public expenditures were devoted to health care in China in 2001. However, about 80 percent of the health and medical care services are concentrated in cities, and timely medical care is not available to more than 100 million people in rural areas. To offset this imbalance, in 2005 China set out a five-year plan to invest 20 billion renminbi (RMB; US$2.4 billion) to rebuild the rural medical service system composed of village clinics and township- and county-level hospitals.

In 2004 health officials announced that China had some 120 million hepatitis B virus carriers. Although not identified until later, China's first case of a new, highly contagious disease, severe acute respiratory syndrome (SARS), occurred in Guangdong in November 2002, and within three months the Ministry of Health reported 300 SARS cases and five deaths in the province. By May 2003, some 8,000 cases of SARS had been reported worldwide; about 66 percent of the cases and 349 deaths occurred in China alone. By early summer 2003, the SARS epidemic had ceased. A vaccine was developed and first-round testing on human volunteers completed in 2004.

China, similar to other nations with migrant and socially mobile populations, has experienced increased incidences of human immunodeficiency virus/acquired immune deficiency syndrome (HIV/AIDS). Based on 2003 estimates, China is believed to have a 0.1 percent adult prevalence rate for HIV/AIDS, one of the lowest rates in the world and especially in Asia. However, because of China's large population, this figure converted in 2003 to some 840,000 cases (more than Russia but fewer than the United States and second in Asia to India), of whom 44,000 died. About 80 percent of those infected live in rural areas. In November 2004, the head of the United Nations AIDS program (UNAIDS) cited China, along with India and Russia, as being on the "tipping point" of having small, localized AIDS epidemics that could turn into major ones capable of hindering the world's efforts to stop the spread of the disease. In 2004 the Ministry of Health reported that its annual AIDS prevention funding had increased from US$1.8 million in 2001 to US$47.1 by 2003 and that, whereas treatment had been restricted to a few hospitals in major cities, treatment was becoming more widely available. According to the study by the World Health Organization, China's Ministry of Health, and UNAIDS, China had an estimated 650,000 people who were infected with HIV by the end of 2005.

In the 2000–2002 period, China had one of the highest per capita caloric intakes in Asia, second only to South Korea and higher than countries such as Japan, Malaysia, and Indonesia. By 2002, 92 percent of the urban population and 68 percent of the rural population had access to an improved water supply, and 69 percent of the urban population and 29 percent of the rural population had access to improved sanitation facilities.

Welfare: In pre-reform China, the socialist state fulfilled the needs of society from cradle to grave. Child care, education, job placement, housing, subsistence, health care, and elder care were largely the responsibility of the work unit as administered through state-owned enterprises and agricultural communes and collectives. As those systems disappeared or were reformed, the "iron rice bowl" approach to social security changed. Article 14 of the constitution stipulates that the state "builds and improves a social security system that corresponds with the level of economic development." In 2004 China experienced the greatest decrease in its poorest population since 1999. People with a per capita income of less than 668 renminbi (RMB; US$80.71) decreased 2.9 million or 10 percent; those with a per capita income of no more than 924 RMB (US$111.64) decreased by 6.4 million or 11.4 percent, according to statistics from the State Council's Poverty Reduction Office. Social security reforms since the late 1990s have included unemployment insurance, medical insurance, workers' compensation insurance, maternity benefits, communal pension funds, and individual pension accounts.

ECONOMY

Overview: After more than a quarter century of reform and opening to the outside world, by 2005 China's economy had become the second largest in the world after the United States when measured on a purchasing power parity (PPP) basis. The government has a goal of quadrupling the gross domestic product (GDP) by 2020 and more than doubling the per capita GDP. Central planning has been curtailed, and widespread market economy mechanisms and a reduced government role have prevailed since 1978. The government fosters a dual economic structure that has evolved from a socialist, centrally planned economy to a socialist market economic system, or a "market economy with socialist characteristics." Industry is marked by increasing technological advancements and productivity. People's communes were eliminated by 1984—after more than 25 years—and the system of township-collective-household production was introduced to the agricultural sector. Private ownership of production assets is legal, although some nonagricultural and industrial facilities are still state-owned and centrally planned. Restraints on foreign trade were relaxed when China acceded to the World Trade Organization in 2001. Joint ventures are encouraged, especially in the coastal special economic zones and open coastal cities. A sign of the affluence that the reformed economy has brought to China might be seen in the number of its millionaires (measured in U.S. dollars): a reported 236,000 millionaires in 2004, an increase of 12 percent over two years earlier.

Chinese officials cite two major trends that have an effect on China's market economy and future development: world multipolarization and regional integration. In relation to these trends, they foresee the roles of China and the United States in world affairs and with one another as very important. Despite successes, China's leaders face a variety of challenges to the nation's future economic development. They have to maintain a high growth rate, deal effectively with the rural workforce, improve the financial system, continue to reform the state-owned enterprises, foster the productive private sector, establish a social security system, improve scientific and educational development, promote better international cooperation, and change the role of the government in the economic system. Despite constraints the international market has placed on China, it nevertheless became the world's third largest trading nation in 2004 after only the United States and Germany.

The Fifth Plenum of the Sixteenth CCP Central Committee took place in October 2005. The Fifth Plenum approved the new Eleventh Five-Year Plan (2006–10), which emphasizes a shift from extensive to intensive growth in order to meet demands for improved economic returns; the conservation of resources to include a 20-percent reduction in energy consumption by 2010; and an effort to raise profitability. Better coordination of urban and rural development and of development between nearby regions also is emphasized in the new plan.

Gross Domestic Product (GDP)/Purchasing Power Parity (PPP): In 2005 China had a GDP of US$2.2 trillion. China's PPP was estimated for 2005 at nearly US$8.9 trillion. PPP per capita in 2005 was estimated at US$6,800. Based on official Chinese data, the estimated GDP growth rate for 2005 was 9.9 percent.

Government Budget: The state budget for 2004 was US$330.6 billion in revenue and US$356.8 billion in expenditures. In the revenue column, 95.5 percent was from taxes and tariffs, 54.9 percent of which was collected by the central government and 45 percent by local authorities. The expenditures were for culture, education, science, and health care (18 percent); capital construction (12 percent); administration (14 percent); national defense (7.7 percent); agriculture, forestry, and water conservancy (5.9 percent); subsidies to compensate for price increases (2.7 percent); pensions and social welfare (1.9 percent); promotion of innovation, science, and technology (4.3 percent); operating expenses of industry, transport, and commerce (1.2 percent); geological prospecting (0.4 percent), and other (31.9 percent). The overall budget deficit in 2004 was approximately US$26 billion, an amount equivalent to about 1.5 percent of gross domestic product (GDP).

Inflation: China's annual rate of inflation averaged 6 percent per year during the 1990–2002 period. Although consumer prices declined by 0.8 percent in 2002, they increased by 1.2 percent in 2003. China's estimated inflation rate in 2005 was 1.8 percent.

Special and Open Economic Zones: As part of its economic reforms and policy of opening to the world, between 1980 and 1984 China established special economic zones (SEZs) in Shantou, Shenzhen, and Zhuhai in Guangdong Province and Xiamen in Fujian Province and designated the entire island province of Hainan a special economic zone. In 1984 China opened 14 other coastal cities to overseas investment (listed north to south): Dalian, Qinhuangdao, Tianjin, Yantai, Qingdao, Lianyungang, Nantong, Shanghai, Ningbo, Wenzhou, Fuzhou, Guangzhou, Zhanjiang, and Beihai. Then, beginning in 1985, the central government expanded the coastal area by establishing the following open economic zones (listed north to south): Liaodong Peninsula, Hebei Province (which surrounds Beijing and Tianjin), Shandong Peninsula, Yangzi River Delta, Xiamen-Zhangzhou-Quanzhou Triangle in southern Fujian Province, Zhujiang (Pearl River) Delta, and Guangxi Zhuang Autonomous Region. In 1990 the Chinese government decided to open the Pudong New Zone in Shanghai to overseas investment, as well as more cities in the Yangzi River Valley. Since 1992 the State Council has opened a number of border cities and all the capital cities of inland provinces and autonomous regions. In addition, 15 free-trade zones, 32 state-level economic and technological development zones, and 53 new- and high-tech industrial development zones have been established in large and medium-sized cities. As a result, a multilevel diversified pattern of opening and integrating coastal areas with river, border, and inland areas has been formed in China.

Agriculture, Forestry, and Fishing: China traditionally has struggled to feed its large population. Even in the twentieth century, famines periodically ravaged China's population. Great emphasis has always been put on agricultural production, but weather, wars, and politics often mitigated good intentions. With the onset of reforms in the late 1970s, the relative share of agriculture in the gross domestic product (GDP) began to increase annually. Driven by sharp rises in prices paid for crops and a trend toward privatization in agriculture, agricultural output increased from 30 percent of GDP in 1980 to 33 percent of GDP by 1983. Since then, however, agriculture has decreased its share in the economy at the same time that the services sector has increased. By 2004 agriculture (including forestry and fishing) produced only 15.2 percent of China's GDP but still is huge by any measure. Some 46.9 percent of the total national workforce was engaged in agriculture, forestry, and fishing in 2004.

According to United Nations statistics, China's cereal production is the largest in the world. In 2003 China produced 377 million tons, or 18.1 percent of total world production. Its plant oil crops—at 15 million tons in 2003—are a close second to those of the United States and amounted to 12.6 percent of total world production. More specifically, China's principal crops in 2004 were rice (176 million tons), corn (132 million tons), sweet potatoes (105 million tons), wheat (91 million tons), sugarcane (89 million tons), and potatoes (70 million tons). Other grains, such as barley, buckwheat, millet, oats, rye, sorghum, and tritcale (a wheat-rye hybrid), added substantially to overall grain production. Crops of peanuts, rapeseed, soybeans, and sugar beets also were significant, as was vegetable production in 2004. Among the highest levels of production were cabbages, tomatoes, cucumbers, and dry onions. In 2004 fruit production also became a significant aspect of the agricultural market. China produced large crops of watermelons, cantaloupes, and other melons that year. Other significant orchard products were apples, citrus fruits, bananas, and mangoes. China, a nation of numerous cigarette smokers, also produced 2.4 million tons of tobacco leaves.

Fertilizer use was a major contributor to these abundant harvests. In 2002 China consumed 25.4 million tons of nitrogenous fertilizers, or 30 percent of total world consumption and more than double the consumption of other major users such as India and the United States in the same period. Among the less used fertilizers, China also was a leader. It consumed 9.9 million tons of phosphate fertilizers (29.5 percent of the world total) and 4.2 million tons of potash fertilizers (18.2 percent of the world total).

With China's accession to the World Trade Organization (WTO) in 2001, food export opportunities have developed that have brought about still more efficient farming techniques. As a result, traditional areas such as grain production have decreased in favor of cash crops of vegetables and fruit for domestic and export trade.

China's livestock herds are the largest in the world, far outstripping all of Europe combined and about comparable in size to all African nations combined. For example, in 2003 China had 49.1 percent of the world's pigs, 22.5 percent of the world's goats, and 7.5 percent of the world's cattle. Converted into food production, China's major livestock products in 2004 were pork (47.2 million tons), poultry eggs (28.0 million tons), cow's milk (18.5 million tons), poultry meat (13.4 million tons), and beef and veal (6.4 million tons). Other meats of significant amounts were mutton, lamb, and goat. Major by-products were cattle hides (1.6 million tons), sheepskins (321,000 tons), and goatskins (375,000 tons). Honey (300,000 tons) and raw silk (95,000 tons) also were major products destined for the commercial market.

Forestry products, measured in annual roundwood production, also abound. In 2004 China produced an estimated 284 million cubic meters of roundwood, the world's third largest supplier after the United States and India, or about 8.5 percent of total world production. From the roundwood, some 11.3 million cubic meters of sawnwood are produced annually.

China also leads the world in fish production. In 2003 it caught 16.7 million tons of fish, far outcatching the second-ranked nation, the United States, with its 4.9 million tons. Aquaculture also was substantial in world terms. In the same year, China harvested 28.8 million tons of fish, an amount more than 10 times that of the second-ranked nation, India, which produced 2.2 million tons. The total fish production in 2003 was 45.6 million tons. Of this total, 63.2 percent was from aquaculture, an increasing sector, and 36.7 percent from fish caught in rivers, lakes, and the sea.

Mining and Minerals: Mineral resources include large reserves of coal and iron ore, plus adequate to abundant supplies of nearly all other industrial minerals. Besides being a major coal producer, China is the world's fifth largest producer of gold and in the early twenty-first century became an important producer and exporter of rare metals needed in high-technology industries. The rare earth reserves at the Bayan Obi mine in Inner Mongolia are thought to be the largest in any single location in the world. Outdated mining and ore-processing technologies are being replaced with modern techniques, but China's rapid industrialization requires imports of minerals from abroad. In particular, iron ore imports from Australia and the United States have soared in the early 2000s as steel production rapidly outstripped domestic iron ore production.

The major areas of production in 2004 were coal (nearly 2 billion tons), iron ore (310 million tons), crude petroleum (175 million tons), natural gas (41 million cubic meters), antimony ore (110,000 tons), tin concentrates (110,000 tons), nickel ore (64,000 tons), tungsten concentrates (67,000 tons), unrefined salt (37 million tons), vanadium (40,000 tons), and molybdenum ore (29,000 tons). In order of magnitude, bauxite, gypsum, barite, magnesite, talc and related minerals, manganese ore, fluorspar, and zinc also were important. In addition, China produced 2,450 tons of silver and 215 tons of gold in 2004. The mining sector accounted for less than 0.9 percent of total employment in 2002 but produced about 5.3 percent of total industrial production.

Industry and Manufacturing: Industry and construction produced 53.1 percent of China's gross domestic product (GDP) in 2005. Industry (including mining, manufacturing, construction, and power) contributed 52.9 percent of GDP in 2004 and occupied 22.5 percent of the workforce. The manufacturing sector produced 44.1 percent of GDP in 2004 and accounted for 11.3 percent of total employment in 2002. China is the world's leading manufacturer of chemical fertilizers, cement, and steel. Prior to 1978, most output was produced by state-owned enterprises. As a result of the economic reforms that followed, there was a significant increase in production by enterprises sponsored by local governments, especially townships and villages, and, increasingly, by private entrepreneurs and foreign investors. By 2002 the share in gross industrial output by state-owned and state-holding industries had decreased to 41 percent, and the state-owned companies themselves contributed only 16 percent of China's industrial output.

An example of an emerging heavy industry is automobile manufacture, which has soared during the reform period. In 1975 only 139,800 automobiles were produced annually, but by 1985 production had reached 443,377, then jumped to nearly 1.1 million by 1992 and increased fairly evenly each year up until 2001, when it reached 2.3 million. In 2002 production rose to nearly 3.3 million and then jumped again the next year to 4.4 million. Domestic sales have kept pace with production. After respectable annual increases in the mid- and late 1990s, sales soared in the early 2000s, reaching 3 million automobiles sold in 2003. With some governmental controls in place, sales dipped to 2.4 million sold in 2004. Some forecasters expect sales to reach 6.9 million by 2015. By 2010 China's automobile production is projected to reach 9.4 million, and the country could become the number-one automaker in the world by 2020. So successful has China's automotive industry been that it began exporting car parts in 1999. China began to plan major moves into the automobile and components export business starting in 2005. A new Honda factory in Guangzhou was being built in 2004 solely for the export market and was expected to ship 30,000 passenger vehicles to Europe in 2005. By 2004, 12 major foreign automotive manufacturers had joint-venture plants in China. They produced a wide range of automobiles, minivans, sport utility vehicles, buses, and trucks. In 2003 China exported US\$4.7 billion worth of vehicles and components, an increase of 34.4 percent over 2002. By 2004 China had become the world's fourth largest automotive vehicle manufacturer.

Concomitant with automotive production and other steel-consuming industries, China has been rapidly increasing its steel production. Iron ore production kept pace with steel production in the early 1990s but was soon outpaced by imported iron ore and other metals in the early 2000s. Steel production, an estimated 140 million tons in 2000, was expected to reach more than 350 million tons a year by 2010.

Energy: As with other economic categories, China is a major producer and consumer of energy resources. In 2002, the most recent year available for United Nations statistics, China produced 934.2 million tons of oil equivalent and consumed 889.6 million tons. Per capita consumption was 687 kilograms, only a quarter of North Korea's estimated consumption, a third of that in Hong Kong, and well below the average for Asia. China's energy consumption has risen dramatically since the inception of its economic reform program in the late 1970s. Electric power generation—mostly by coal-burning plants—has been in particular demand; China's electricity use in the 1990s increased by between 3 percent and 7 percent per year. In 2003 electricity use increased by 15 percent over the previous year, and supplies could not keep up with demand, thus slowing economic development. Government statistics indicate that the overall demand for electric power for 2004 was projected to be around 2 trillion kilowatt-hours, but by June of that year a 60-billion kilowatt-hour shortfall had been projected. Energy production failed to keep up with industrial demand, resulting in power cutoffs throughout most of the country. In 2005 the Chinese Communist Party expressed the determination to reduce energy consumption by 20 percent per capita of the gross domestic product (GDP) by 2010.

China is largely self-sufficient in all energy forms. Its coal production is the highest in the world. Some 75.6 percent of China's energy was produced from coal in 2004. The coal reserves are among the world's largest, and mining technology has been improving since the 1990s. Coal has even been exported since the early 1970s.

Petroleum fulfilled 13.5 percent and natural gas 3.0 percent of China's energy requirements in 2004. The petroleum reserves are large, of varying quality, and in disparate locations. There are oil deposit blocks in the northwest and offshore tracts believed to be among the world's largest. In December 2004, it was reported that some 20.5 billion tons of oil reserves had been discovered in North China's Bohai Bay and more than 20 billion tons in Xinjiang's Tarim Basin. There also are an estimated 28 billion cubic meters of natural gas in Xinjiang, 100 billion cubic meters in Sichuan, and 200 million cubic meters in Inner Mongolia, as well as substantial natural gas reserves offshore. Even though it has exported petroleum since the early 1970s, China, nevertheless, is a net importer of crude petroleum because the required high grades of petroleum are not available domestically. Imports of mineral fuels totaled 6.6 percent of the cost of total imports in 2002. In 2004 Russia agreed to expand its oil exports to China. With deliveries sent by railroad, the two countries expected oil deliveries to China to reach 10 million tons in 2005 and 15 million tons in 2006. However, China's total petroleum imports were expected to exceed 100 million tons in 2005.

China's hydroelectric potential is the greatest in the world and the sixth largest in capacity. However, in 2004 hydroelectric power produced only 7.9 percent of China's energy needs. The Three Gorges hydropower project in Hubei Province on the Yangzi River started delivering power to eastern and central provinces in July 2003 and is expected to produce 84.7 billion kilowatt-hours per year when the project is completed by 2009. The main wall of the dam was completed in 2006, two years ahead of schedule.

Construction: As might be expected in a rapidly developing nation, China's construction sector has grown substantially since the early 1980s. In the twenty-first century, investment in capital construction has experienced major annual increases. In 2001 investments increased 8.5 percent over the previous year. In 2002 there was a 16.4 percent increase, followed by a 30 percent increase in 2003.

Services: In 2005 the services sector produced 40.3 percent of China's gross domestic product. Prior to the onset of economic reforms in 1978, China's services sector was characterized by state-operated shops, rationing, and regulated prices. With reform came private markets and individual entrepreneurs and a comparatively free-wheeling commercial sector. Urban areas now are filled with shopping malls and dotted with Western-style retail shops and fast-food chains. An array of Western-style fast-food chains, trendy restaurants, night clubs, and consumer shops of all kinds operate within close proximity to Mao Zedong's mausoleum in Beijing. Other east coast cities have followed suit, and several cities in the interior are not far behind. If anything, as the Economist Intelligence Unit points out, the retail sector "suffers from oversupply." Joint-venture hotels abound in China's major cities.

Banking and Finance: Banking reform was initiated in China in 1994, and the Commercial Banking Law took effect in July 1995. The aims of these actions were to strengthen the role of the central bank—the People's Bank of China—and to allow private banks to be established. The People's Bank of China was established in 1948. It issues China's currency and implements the nation's monetary policies. China's oldest bank, founded in 1908, is the Bank of Communications Limited, a commercial enterprise located in Shanghai. China's second oldest bank was established in 1912 as the Bank of China. Since 2004 it has become a shareholding company known as the Bank of China Limited and handles foreign exchange and international financial settlements. The Agricultural Bank of China, founded in 1951, is mainly involved in rural financing and the provision of services to agricultural, industrial, commercial, and transportation enterprises in rural areas. Other major banks include the China Construction Bank; established in 1954 as the People's Construction Bank of China, it has been a state-owned commercial bank since 1994 and maintains some 15,400 business outlets inside and outside

China, including six overseas branches and two overseas representative offices. The China Construction Bank was restructured in 2003 into a shareholding bank called the China Construction Bank Corporation, with the state holding the controlling shares. The China International Trust and Investment Corporation was founded in 1979 to assist economic and technological cooperation, finance, banking, investment, and trade. The Industrial and Commercial Bank of China was founded in 1984 to handle industrial and commercial credits and international business. The Agricultural Development Bank of China, Export and Import Bank of China, and State Development Bank all were founded in 1994. China's first private commercial national bank, the China Minsheng Banking Corporation, was opened in 1996. Commercial banks are supervised by the China Banking Regulatory Commission, which was established in 2003. In 2005 the commission announced the launching of a new postal savings bank to replace the old system and its more than 36,000 outdated outlets nationwide.

When first permitted in the mid-1980s, foreign banks were restricted to designated cities and could deal only with transactions by foreign companies in China. After those restrictions were loosened following China's accession to the World Trade Organization in 2001, some foreign banks have been allowed to provide services to local residents and businesses. In 2004 there were some 70 foreign banks with more than 150 branches in China.

There are stock exchanges in Beijing, Shanghai (the third largest in the world), and Shenzhen and futures exchanges in Shanghai, Dalian, and Zhengzhou. They are regulated by the China Securities Regulatory Commission.

Tourism: China has become a major tourist destination, especially since its opening to the world in the late 1970s. By 2003 China had some 9,751 tourist hotels and a burgeoning hospitality industry, much of it joint ventures with foreign partners. In 2004 China received some 109 million tourists and visitors. However, 88.4 million (80.7 percent of the total) visits were made by individuals arriving via the Hong Kong and Macau special administrative regions, including those who made multiple and often same-day trips to China. Others came from Taiwan (3.3 percent), Japan (3.0 percent), South Korea (2.6 percent), Russia, (1.6 percent), and the United States (nearly 1.1 percent). In 2004 visitors to China spent some US$25.7 billion. At the same time, China increased its own tourism; travelers from China spent more than US$15 billion on tourism in other countries in 2002.

Labor: China's estimated employed labor force in 2005 totaled 791.4 million persons. During 2003, 49 percent of the labor force worked in agriculture, forestry, and fishing; 22 percent in mining, manufacturing, energy, and construction industries; and 29 percent in the services sector and other categories. In 2004 some 25 million persons were employed by 743,000 private enterprises. The All-China Federation of Trade Unions (ACFTU) is the state-sanctioned labor organization with which other official labor organizations affiliate. The ACFTU was established in 1925 to represent the interests of national and local trade unions and trade union councils. The ACFTU reported a membership of 130 million, out of an estimated 248 million urban workers, at the end of 2002. An independent trade union group, the Workers' Autonomous Federation, was founded in 1989 but fell short of its goal of establishing a separate trade union movement when many of its leaders were arrested during the June 1989 Tiananmen incident.

Official Chinese statistics reveal that 4.2 percent of the total urban workforce was unemployed in 2004, although the true figure was believed by outside observers to be 10 percent. As part of its newly developing social security legislation, China has an unemployment insurance system. At the end of 2003, more than 103.7 million people were participating in the plan, and 7.4 million laid-off employees had received benefits.

Foreign Economic Relations: The government traditionally has decided the composition of China's foreign trade. However, since the initiation of reforms in 1978, increasing numbers of private partnerships have developed, and trade is primarily dictated by the marketplace. After years of disagreement over trade practices with its largest export partner, the United States, China agreed to a range of economic reforms designed to open Chinese markets to private and foreign investment. Subsequently, the U.S. Congress granted China permanent most-favored-nation status in 2000. In 2001 China acceded to the World Trade Organization. As a result of its efforts in the global marketplace, by 2004 China had become the world's third largest trading power behind the United States and Germany.

Imports: China's imports rose by 36 percent in 2004, totaling US$561.4 billion. Of these imports, the major components were machinery and equipment, mineral fuels, plastics, and iron and steel. The major trading partners were Japan (16.8 percent), Taiwan (11.4 percent), South Korea (11.1 percent), and the United States (8 percent). The 2004 amount reflected the rising trend in imports during the pervious seven years. In 1996 China's imports totaled US$138.8 billion and reached US$225 billion by 2000.

Exports: China's exports rose by 35.4 percent in 2004, totaling US$593.4 billion and favoring machinery and equipment, textiles and clothing, footwear, toys, and mineral fuels as the major commodities. The primary trading partners were the United States (21.1percent), Hong Kong (trading as a separate economy, mostly for re-export purposes, 17 percent), Japan (12.4 percent), and South Korea (4.7 percent). One of the burgeoning exports, toys (both unsophisticated and high-tech, of which China provides about 75 percent of the total worldwide), also has a growing domestic market (US$6 billion a year). The 2004 total reflected the rising trend in exports during the previous seven years, increasing from US$151 billion in 1996 and reaching US$249.2 billion by 2000.

Trade Balance: China had a favorable trade balance of US$32 billion in 2004 and US$38.7 billion in 2003. These amounts reflect the general course of a favorable trade balance during the pervious eight years. In 1996 China's trade balance was US$12.2 billion, peaking at US$43.4 billion in 1998 but declining to US$24.1 billion by 2000 before starting its new increase.

Balance of Payments: China's current account balance in 2004 was nearly US$68.7 billion. Added to this total was US$54.9 billion in foreign direct investment (exceeding that invested in the United States). When other investments, assets, and liabilities are brought into the calculation, the overall balance of payments was US$206.1 billion in 2004, compared with US$75.2 billion in 2002 and US$116.5 billion in 2003.

External Debt: According to United Nations statistics for 2001, China's external and public, or publicly guaranteed, long-term debt had reached US$91.7 billion. China's debt had grown steadily during the 1990s, peaked at US$112.8 billion in 1997, and then declined annually thereafter. By 2004 China had US$618.5 billion in its international reserve account, 98.6 percent of which was from foreign exchange, not including the Bank of China's foreign exchange holdings.

Foreign Aid and Foreign Investment: China is the recipient of bilateral and multilateral official development assistance and official aid to individual recipients. In 2003 it received US$1.3 billion in such disbursements, or about US$1 per capita. This total was down from the 1999 figures of US$2.4 billion and US$1.90 per capita. Some of this aid comes to China in the form of socioeconomic development assistance through the United Nations (UN) system. China received US$112 million in such UN assistance annually in 2001 and 2002, the largest portion coming from the UN Development Programme (UNDP).

China also obtains foreign capital through foreign loans, direct foreign investment (FDI), and other investment by foreign businesses. Since 1980 foreign businesses from more than 170 countries and regions have invested in Chinese joint-venture enterprises. Most joint-venture activities are located in coastal cities and increasing numbers in inland cities as well. Some 300 of the 500 top transnational companies in the world have invested in China, and foreign investments have become an important capital source for China's economic development. In 1999 FDI totaled US$40.3 billion. Between 1979 and 1999, cumulative FDI totaled US$305.9 billion, US$40.3 billion of which was invested in 1999 alone. In that year, China had approved the establishment of 342,000 foreign-funded enterprises, more than 100,000 of which have gone into operation. Contracted FDI reached nearly US$82.8 billion in 2002, US$115 billion in 2003, US$153.48 in 2004, and US$130.33 billion in the first nine months of 2005.

Currency and Exchange Rate: China's currency is the renminbi (RMB, people's currency) or yuan. The interbank exchange rate on August 1, 2006, was US$1=RMB7.98. The RMB is made up of 100 fen or 10 jiao. Coins are issued in denominations of one, two, and five fen; one and five jiao, and one RMB. Banknotes are issued in denominations of one, two, and five jiao; and one, two, five, 10, 50, and 100 RMB.

Fiscal Year: Calendar Year.

TRANSPORTATION AND TELECOMMUNICATIONS

Overview: Transportation networks have experienced major growth and expansion since 1949 and especially since the early 1980s. Railroads, which are the primary mode of transportation, have doubled in length since the mid-twentieth century, and an extensive network provides sufficient service to the entire nation. Even Tibet with its remote location and seemingly insurmountable terrain has railroad service under construction. The larger cities have subway systems in operation, under construction, or in the planning stage. The highway and road system also has gone through rapid expansion, resulting in a rapid increase of motor vehicle use throughout China.

Roads: In 2005 China had a total road network of more than 3.3 million kilometers, although approximately 1.47 million kilometers of this network are classified as "village roads." Paved roads totaled 770,265 kilometers in 2004; the remainder were gravel, improved earth standard, or merely earth tracks. Highways (totaling 130,000 kilometers) were critical to China's economic growth as it worked to mitigate a poor distribution network and authorities sought to spur economic activity directly. All major cities are expected to be linked with a 55,000-kilometer interprovince expressway system by 2020. The highway and road systems carried nearly 11.6 billion tons of freight and 769.6 trillion passenger/kilometers in 2003. The importance of highways and motor vehicles, which carry 13.5 percent of cargo and 49.1 percent of passengers, was growing rapidly in the mid-2000s. Road usage has increased significantly, as automobiles, including privately owned vehicles, rapidly replace bicycles as the popular vehicle of choice in China. In 2002, excluding military and probably internal security vehicles, there were 12 million passenger cars and buses in operation and 8.1 million other vehicles. In 2003 China reported that 23.8 million vehicles were used for business purposes, including 14.8 million passenger vehicles and 8.5 million trucks. The latest statistics from the Beijing Municipal Statistics Bureau show that Beijing had nearly 1.3 million privately owned cars at the end of 2004 or 11 for each 100 Beijing residents. Beijing currently has the highest annual rate of private car growth.

Railroads: Railroads are the major mode of transportation in China. Carrying some 24 percent of the world's railroad transportation volume, China's railroads are critical to its economy. Because of its limited capital, overburdened infrastructure, and need to continually modernize, the rail system, which is controlled by the Ministry of Railways through a network of regional divisions, operates on an austere budget. Foreign capital investment in the freight sector was allowed beginning in 2003, and international public stock offerings are to be opened in 2006. In another move to better capitalize and reform the railroad system, the Ministry of Railways established three public shareholder-owned companies in 2003: China Railways Container Transport Company, China Railway Special Cargo Service Company, and China Railways Parcel Express Company.

The national rail system is modernizing and expanding rapidly and is efficient within the limits of the available track. Some 71,898 kilometers of track were operational in 2002. This total included 71, 898 kilometers of 1.435-meter gauge (18,115 kilometers of which were electrified) and 3,600 kilometers of 1.000-meter and 0.750-meter gauge local industrial lines. There were an additional 23,945 kilometers of dual-gauge track not included in the total. As of 2002, some 23,058 kilometers of the railroad routes were double tracked, representing 38.7 percent of the total. In 2004 China's railroad inventory included 15,456 locomotives owned by the national railroad system. The inventory in recent times included some 100 steam locomotives, but the last such locomotive, built in 1999, is now in service as a tourist attraction while the others have been retired from commercial service. The remaining locomotives are either diesel- or electric-powered. Another 352 locomotives are owned by local railroads and 604 operated by joint-venture railroads. National railroad freight cars numbered 520,101 and passenger coaches 39,766. In 2003 China's railroads carried 2.2 trillion tons of freight and 478.9 trillion passenger/kilometers. Only India had more passenger/kilometers and the United States more net ton/kilometers than China.

In October 2005, China completed a new section of the Qinghai-Tibet Railway, a 1,142-kilometer-long section between Golmud and Lhasa. When it goes into full service in late 2006 or early 2007, the 1,956 kilometer-long line, which began construction in 1984, will link the rest of China with Tibet via a hub at Xining in Qinghai Province. Another large-scale railroad project is the New Silk Road or Eurasian Continental Bridge project that was launched in 1992. In China the project involves the modernization and infrastructure development of a 4,131-kilometer-long railroad route starting in Lianyungang, Jiangsu Province, and traveling through central and northwestern China to Urumqi, Xinjiang Uygur Autonomous Region, to the Alataw Pass into Kazakhstan. From that point, the railroad links to some 6,800 kilometers of routes that end in Rotterdam. China also has established rail links between seaports and interior export-processing zones. For example, in 2004 Chengdu in Sichuan Province was linked to the Shenzhen Special Economic Zone in coastal Guangdong; exports clear customs in Chengdu and are shipped twice daily by rail to the seaport at Shenzhen for fast delivery.

Rapid Transit: The Beijing metro system, which opened in 1969, has 113 kilometers of subway track on four lines, plus an additional 98 kilometers slated by 2010. The Guangzhou system, which opened in 1999, has 18.5 kilometers and an additional 133 kilometers planned. Shanghai metro, which opened in 1995, has 8 lines, 68 stations, and 82.8 kilometers of track, with an additional 108.4 kilometers under construction or planned. The Tianjin metro was begun in 1970 as a planned network of 153.9 kilometers on seven lines; large sections remain closed for reconstruction, but one 26.2-kilometer-long line opened for trial operations in June 2006. The Shenzhen metro opened in 2004, initially with two lines, 19 stations, and 21.8 kilometers of track. Also under construction are subway and light rail systems in Chongqing and Nanjing, and systems are planned for Chengdu and Qingdao. Metro transit in Hong Kong is covered by the privately operated Mass Transit Railway, which opened in 1979 and now has six metro lines with 50 stations.

China also has the world's first commercial magnetic levitation (maglev) train service. A Sino-German joint venture, 38-kilometer-long route between downtown Shanghai and the Pudong airport opened in 2003. The project cost US$1.2 billion and has experienced an average of 8,000 passengers per day, well below capacity. In 2004 the first Chinese-made maglev train made its debut in Dalian, a major port city in Northeast China's Liaoning Province. The 10.3-meter-long train has a top speed of just under 110 kilometers per hour. Although the cost to build was high at US$6 million per kilometer, China's outlay was still only one-sixth of the world average.

Ports and Shipping: China has more than 2,000 ports, 130 of which are open to foreign ships. The major ports, including river ports accessible by ocean-going ships, are Beihai, Dalian, Dangdong, Fuzhou, Guangzhou, Haikou, Hankou, Huangpu, Jiujiang, Lianyungang, Nanjing, Nantong, Ningbo, Qingdao, Qinhuangdao, Rizhao, Sanya, Shanghai, Shantou, Shenzhen, Tianjin, Weihai, Wenzhou, Xiamen, Xingang, Yangzhou, Yantai, and Zhanjiang. Additionally, Hong Kong is a major international port serving as an important trade center for China. In 2005 Shanghai Port Management Department reported that its Shanghai port became the world's largest cargo port, processing cargo topping 443 million tons and surpassing Singapore's port. As of 2004, China's merchant fleet had 3,497 ships. Of these, 1,700 ships of 1,000 gross registered tons (GRT) or more totaled 20. 4 million tons. In 2003 China's major coastal ports handled 2.1 billion tons of freight.

Inland and Coastal Waterways: China has more than 140,000 kilometers of navigable rivers, streams, lakes, and canals, and in 2003 these inland waterways carried nearly 1.6 trillion tons of freight and 6.3 trillion passenger/kilometers to more than 5,100 inland ports. The main navigable rivers are the Heilongjiang; Yangzi; Xiangjiang, a short branch of the Yangzi; and Zhujiang. Ships of up to 10,000 tons can navigate more than 1,000 kilometers on the Yangzi as far as Wuhan. Ships of 1,000 tons can navigate from Wuhan to Chongqing, another 1,286 kilometers upstream. The Grand Canal is the world's longest canal at 1,794 kilometers and serves 17 cities between Beijing and Hangzhou. It links five major rivers: the Haihe, Huaihe, Huanghe, Qiantang, and Yangzi.

Civil Aviation and Airports: As a result of the rapidly expanding civil aviation industry, by 2005 China had 489 airports of all types and sizes in operation, 389 of which had paved runways and 89 of which had runways of 3,047 meters or shorter. There also were 30 heliports, an increasingly used type of facility. With the additional airports came a proliferation of airlines. In 2002 the government merged the nine largest airlines into three regional groups based in Beijing, Shanghai, and Guangzhou, respectively: Air China, China Eastern Airlines, and China Southern Airlines, which operate most of China's external flights. By 2005 these three had been joined by six other major airlines: Hainan Airlines, Shanghai Airlines, Shandong Airlines, Xiamen Airlines, Shenzhen Airlines, and Sichuan Airlines. Together, these nine airlines had a combined fleet of some 860 aircraft, mostly Boeing from the United States and Airbus from France. To meet growing demands for passenger and cargo capacity, in 2005 these airlines significantly expanded their fleets with orders placed for additional Boeing and Airbus aircraft expected to be delivered by 2010. In June 2006, it was announced that an Airbus A320 assembly plant would be built in the Binhai New Area of Tianjin, with the first aircraft to be delivered in 2008. The Civil Aviation Administration of China (CAAC), also called the General Administration of Civil Aviation of China, was established as a government agency in 1949 to operate China's commercial air fleet. In 1988 CAAC's operational fleet was transferred to new, semiautonomous airlines and has served since as a regulatory agency.

Major airports include the Capital International Airport, located 27 kilometers northeast of central Beijing; two in Shanghai under the control of the Shanghai Airport Authority: Hongqiao International Airport, which is located 13 kilometers west of central Shanghai, and Pudong International Airport, which is located 30 kilometers southeast of central Shanghai; and the new Baiyun International Airport, which opened in August 2004 and is located 28 kilometers from downtown Guangzhou. Other major airports are located at Chengdu, Dalian, Hangzhou, Harbin, Hohhot, Kunming, Qingdao, Shenyang, Tianjin, Urumqi, Xiamen, and Xi'an. Additionally, the Hong Kong International Airport, located at Chek Lap Kok on Lantau Island 34 kilometers northwest of Hong Kong Island. China is served both by numerous major international flights to most countries of the world and a host of domestic regional airlines. In 2003 China's civil aviation sector carried nearly 2.2 million tons of freight and 126.3 trillion passenger/kilometers.

Pipelines: As of 2004, China had 15,890 kilometers of gas pipelines, 14,478 kilometers of oil pipelines, and 3,280 kilometers for refined products. China's pipelines carried 219.9 million tons of petroleum and natural gas in 2003. As a major oil and gas consumer, China is searching for more external supples. Construction of a 4,200-kilometer-long pipeline from Xinjiang to Shanghai was completed in 2004.

Telecommunications: The Ministry of Information Industry reported in 2004 that China had 295 million subscribers to main telephone lines and 305 million cellular telephone subscribers, the highest numbers in both categories in the world but second per capita to the United States. Both categories showed substantial increases over the previous decade; in 1995 there were only 3.6 million cellular telephone subscribers and around 20 million main-line telephone subscribers. By 2003 there were 42 telephones per 100 population. Internet use also has soared in China from about 60,000 Internet users in 1995 to 22.5 million users in 2000; by 2005 the number had reached 103 million. Although this figure is well below the 159 million users in the United States and although fairly low per capita, it was second in the world and on a par with Japan's 57 million users. China's 2.7 million kilometers of optical fiber telecommunication cables by 2003 assisted greatly in the modernization process. China produces an increasing volume of televisions both for domestic use and export. In 2001 China produced more than 46 million televisions and claimed 317 million sets in use. At the same time, there were 417 million radios in use in China, a rate of 342 per 1,000 population. However, many more are reached, especially in rural areas, via loudspeaker broadcasts of radio programs that bring transmissions to large numbers of radioless households.

GOVERNMENT AND POLITICS

Overview: China is a unitary and socialist state whose constitution calls on the nation to "concentrate on socialist modernization by following the road of building socialism with Chinese characteristics" all the while adhering to the "leadership of the Chinese Communist Party (CCP) and the guidance of Marxism-Leninism, Mao Zedong Thought and Deng Xiaoping Theory" as well as "the important thought of the Three Represents," which are attributed to former CCP general secretary and president of China Jiang Zemin. The political system is led by the 66.4-million-member CCP. Political processes are guided by the CCP constitution and, increasingly, by the state constitution, both promulgated in 1982. The CCP constitution was revised in 2002, and the state constitution was amended in 1988, 1993, 1999, and 2004. Both constitutions stress the principle of democratic centralism, under which the representative organs of both party and state are elected by lower bodies and in turn elect their administrative arms at corresponding levels. Within representative and executive bodies, the minority must abide by decisions of the majority; lower bodies obey orders of higher-level organs. In theory, the National Party Congress ranks as the highest organ of party power, but actual power lies in the CCP Central Committee and its even more exclusive Political Bureau. At the apex of all political power are the members of the elite Standing Committee of the Political Bureau.

In September 2004 at the Fourth Plenary Session of the 16th CCP Congress, former party, state, and military leader Jiang Zemin completed his formal handover of responsibilities to Hu Jintao. At the plenum, Jiang gave up his last key position, chairmanship of the CCP Central Military Commission. With Hu holding that position, as well as those of general secretary of the CCP (since November 2002) and president of China (since March 2003), the succession ostensibly was complete. However, Jiang confidants and allies were still entrenched in key positions, and Jiang himself, through several high-profile public appearances, indicated that he would continue to be influential in central party and state policy making.

Executive Branch: The head of state of China is the president (Hu Jintao, since March 2003, when he succeeded Jiang Zemin). The vice president is Zeng Qinghong (since March 2003; he succeeded Hu). Articles 79–80 of the constitution provide for a president and vice president elected by the National People's Congress (NPC) for five-year terms and no more than two consecutive terms. The president "engages in activities involving State affairs and receives foreign diplomatic represents." In pursuance of the decisions of the NPC Standing Committee, the president appoints and recalls plenipotentiary representatives abroad and ratifies and abrogates treaties and important agreements concluded with foreign states. The vice president assists the president in his work, "may exercise such parts of the functions and powers of the President as the President may entrust to him," and succeeds to the presidency should the office of president become vacant. Should both offices become vacant, the chairman of the NPC Standing Committee becomes acting president until the NPC elects a new president and vice president.

The government is led by the State Council, the equivalent of a cabinet. The State Council is headed by a premier (Wen Jiabao, since March 2003). There also are four vice premiers and five state councillors (one of whom is the secretary general of the State Council). One of the vice premiers and two of the state councillors double as ministers handling such key portfolios as national defense, public security, and public health. In 2006 there were 22 ministries and four commissions subordinate to the State Council. In addition, the People's Bank of China (China's central bank) and the National Audit Office are part of the State Council system. The five-year terms of office run concurrently with those of the National People's Congress (NPC) and are limited to no more than two consecutive terms. Executive meetings of the State Council are attended by the premier, vice premiers, state councillors, and secretary general of the State Council. The State Council reports on its work to the NPC and, when the NPC is not in session, to its Standing Committee.

Legislative Branch: According to the constitution, the National People's Congress (NPC) is "the highest organ of state power" and exercises "the legislative power of the state." Deputies to the NPC are elected from the provinces, autonomous regions, centrally administered municipalities, special administrative regions, and the armed forces. Elections are conducted by the permanent body of the NPC, the Standing Committee, and normally are held at least two months before the end of the current NPC. Deputies serve five-year terms and meet annually for two or three weeks, typically in March or April; 2,979 deputies were elected to the current 10th NPC. The NPC is empowered to amend the constitution; supervise the enforcement of the constitution; and elect the president and vice president of the People's Republic, chairman of the state Central Military Commission, president of the Supreme People's Court, and procurator general of the Supreme People's Procuratorate. It also has the authority "to decide on" the choice of the premier of the State Council upon nomination of the president and the members of the State Council upon nomination by the premier. Among the other responsibilities of the NPC is to "examine and approve" national economic and social development plans and the state budget and to "decide on questions of war and peace." The NPC also can alter or annul "inappropriate decisions" of the Standing Committee, approve the establishment of provincial-level units, and rule on the establishment of special administrative regions. The current chairman of the NPC Standing Committee since March 2003 is Wu Bangguo, a former vice premier and current member of the Standing Committee of the Chinese Communist Party (CCP) Political Bureau.

When the full NPC is not in session, its Standing Committee meets and wields broad legislative powers. The NPC Standing Committee consists of a chairman, 15 vice chairmen, a secretary general, and 153 members, including the officers. Standing Committee members are not allowed to hold administrative, judicial, or procuratorial posts and, in practice, are often senior CCP and former state leaders and officials. As with the NPC membership, the chairman and vice chairmen may serve no more than two consecutive terms. Other committees, which work under the direction of the Standing Committee, include Nationalities; Law; Finance and Economic; Education, Science, Culture, and Public Health; Foreign Affairs; Overseas Chinese; and other special committees.

Another quasi-constitutional consultative body that provides an institutional framework for interaction among the CCP, state organizations, and other social and political organizations is the Chinese People's Political Consultative Conference (CPPCC). Members are distinguished scholars, educators, and intellectuals, key representatives of religious and minority nationality groups, leading members of political parties loyal to the CCP during the anti-Guomindang years, and representatives of Hong Kong, Macau, Taiwan, and Chinese overseas. The CPPCC typically meets once a year and has a standing committee that convenes when needed between sessions. The current chairman of the CPPCC is Jia Qinglin, a member of the CCP Political Bureau Standing Committee and ally of former CCP secretary general Jiang Zemin.

Judicial Branch: China has a four-level court system. At the top is the Supreme People's Court in Beijing. Lower courts are the higher people's courts in provinces, autonomous regions, and special municipalities; intermediate people's courts at the prefecture level and also in parts of provinces, autonomous regions, and special municipalities; and basic people's courts in counties, towns, and municipal districts. Special courts handle matters affecting the military, railroad transportation, water transportation, and forestry.

Constitutionally, the court system exercises judicial power independently and technically is free of interference from administrative organs, public organizations, and individuals. The Supreme People's Court supervises the administration of justice by local courts and special courts, while courts at higher levels oversee the administration of courts at lower levels. At each level, the courts are "responsible to the organs of state power which created them." Judges are limited to two consecutive terms running concurrently with the National People's Congress or local people's congresses.

The court system is paralleled by a hierarchy of prosecuting organs called people's procuratorates; at the apex stands the Supreme People's Procuratorate. The procurators serve as prosecutors, or district attorneys, and are limited to two consecutive terms running concurrently with the NPC or local people's congresses.

Administrative Divisions: China has 22 provinces (*sheng*), five autonomous regions (*zizhiqu*), and four municipalities (*shi*). The provinces are, in the northeast: Heilongjiang, Jilin, and Liaoning; in the north: Shandong, Hebei, Shanxi, and Shaanxi; in central China: Jiangsu, Anhui, Henan, Hubei, and Zhejiang; in the south: Hunan, Jiangxi, Fujian, Guangdong, and Hainan (an island in the South China Sea); in the southwest: Guizhou, Yunnan, and Sichuan; and in the northwest: Gansu and Qinghai. The autonomous regions—Guangxi Zhuang, Tibet (Xizang),

Xinjiang Uygur, Inner Mongolia, and Ningxia Hui—are in border areas with large non-Han ethnic minority populations from which they take their names or part of their names. The four municipalities—Beijing, Tianjin, Shanghai, and Chongqing—are directly controlled by the central government. China also has two special administrative regions (SARs): Hong Kong, which reverted from British control in 1997; and Macau, which reverted from Portuguese control in 1999. Beijing also claims Taiwan as a province.

Provincial and Local Government: The governors of China's provinces and autonomous regions and mayors of its centrally controlled municipalities are appointed by the central government in Beijing after receiving the nominal consent of the National People's Congress (NPC). The Hong Kong and Macau special administrative regions (SARs) have some local autonomy since they have separate governments, legal systems, and basic constitutional laws, but they come under Beijing's control in matters of foreign affairs and national security, and their chief executives are handpicked by the central government. Below the provincial level in 2004 there were 50 rural prefectures, 283 prefecture-level cities, 374 county-level cities, 852 county-level districts under the jurisdiction of nearby cities, and 1,636 counties. There also were 662 cities (including those incorporated into the four centrally controlled municipalities), 808 urban districts, and 43,258 township-level regions. Counties are divided into townships and villages. While most have appointed officials running them, some lower-level jurisdictions have direct popular elections. The organs of self-governing ethnic autonomous areas (regions, prefectures, and counties)—people's congresses and people's governments—exercise the same powers as their provincial-level counterparts but are guided additionally by the Law on Regional Ethnic Autonomy and require NPC Standing Committee approval for regulations they enact "in the exercise of autonomy" and "in light of the political, economic, and cultural characteristics of the ethnic group or ethnic groups in the areas."

Special Administrative Regions: China has two special administrative regions, Hong Kong (Xianggang in Putonghua) and Macau (Aomen in Putonghua). As a result of the First Anglo-Chinese War (1842), China ceded Hong Kong Island to the United Kingdom under the Treaty of Nanjing in 1842. In 1860 the British acquired in perpetuity the Kowloon (Jiulong) Peninsula under the Convention of Beijing. The remaining area, the New Territories, was leased for 99 years in 1898. The Sino-British Joint Declaration on the Question of Hong Kong was signed between the Chinese and British Governments in 1984. The entire colony was returned to Chinese sovereignty in 1997 as the Hong Kong Special Administrative Region (SAR). Although originally the 1,092-square-kilometer area was part of Guangdong Province, the Hong Kong SAR reports directly to the State Council in Beijing. The head of state of Hong Kong is the president of China, Hu Jintao. The head of government is a Beijing appointee, Chief Executive Tung Chee-hwa. Hong Kong, with an estimated 6,940,432 people (as of July 2006), has a partly popularly elected legislature and operates under the Basic Law, which embodies the principle of "one country, two systems" and states that the socialist system and policies shall not be practiced in Hong Kong; Hong Kong's previous capitalist system and lifestyle are to remain unchanged until 2047. The Basic Law of the Hong Kong SAR was adopted on April 4, 1990, by the National People's Congress (NPC) and came into effect on July 1, 1997. Chinese and English are the official languages of Hong Kong.

The area that has come to be called Macau had been a maritime way station between China and India and regions farther west since the early sixteenth century. Portugal first obtained a leasehold on the area from the Qing court in 1557, although China retained sovereignty. In 1844, without Beijing's concurrence, Lisbon made Macau an overseas province of Portugal. Although China recognized Macau as a Portuguese colony in an 1862 treaty signed with Portugal, the treaty was never ratified by China, and Macau was never officially ceded to Portugal. A protocol dealing with relations between China and Portugal was signed in Lisbon in 1887 confirming the "perpetual occupation and government" of Macau by Portugal (with Portugal's promise "never to alienate Macau and dependencies without agreement with China"). The islands of Taipa and Coloane also were ceded to Portugal, but the border of the Macau Peninsula with the mainland was not delimited. The Treaty of Commerce and Friendship (1888) recognized Portuguese sovereignty over Macau but again was never actually ratified by China. In 1974 the new Portuguese government granted independence to all overseas colonies and recognized Macau as part of China's territory. In 1979 China and Portugal exchanged diplomatic recognition, and Beijing acknowledged Macau as "Chinese territory under Portuguese administration." A joint communiqué signed in 1986 called for negotiations on the Macau question, and four rounds of talks followed between June 30, 1986, and March 26, 1987. The Joint Declaration on the Question of Macau was signed in Beijing on April 13, 1987, setting the stage for the return of Macau to full Chinese sovereignty as a special administrative region on December 20, 1999.

Although originally the now 28.2-square-kilometer area was part of Guangdong Province, the Macau SAR reports directly to the State Council in Beijing. Macau's head of state is the president of China. The head of government is a Beijing appointee, Chief Executive Edmund H.W. Ho. Macau, numbering an estimated 453,125 people (in July 2006), also has a partly popularly elected legislature and operates under the Basic Law of the Macau SAR, adopted by the NPC in 1993 and taking effect on December 20, 1999. Like the Basic Law of the Hong Kong SAR, Macau's basic law covers the relationship between the central government and Macau; the fundamental rights and duties of the residents; the political structure; the economy and cultural and social affairs; external affairs; and the amendment process. Chinese and Portuguese are the official languages of Macau.

Cross-Strait Relations with Taiwan: China considers Taiwan a province and an inalienable part of China, which has been separated from China since 1949 when the Guomindang (Nationalist Party) government of Jiang Jieshi (Chiang Kei-shek) fled there in the face of defeat by communist forces. Taiwan still controls one island that appertains to the mainland—Jinmen (Kinmen or Quemoy), which is part of Fujian Province. In Beijing matters dealing with Taiwan are handled by the Chinese Communist Party (CCP) Central Committee's Taiwan Work Office and the State Council's Taiwan Affairs Office. Beijing is adamantly opposed to independence or any quasi-state status for Taiwan and has alternated since the late 1970s between overtures for peaceful reunification and statements of resolution to forcefully reclaim Taiwan if necessary. Beijing has called for resuming cross-strait negotiations, formally ending the state of hostility that has persisted since 1949, and addressing cross-strait problems through timely negotiations. During the reform period, China and Taiwan began to allow economic and trade exchanges, travel, tourism, and other activities. Several breakthroughs in relations occurred in 2005. The first was the launch of two-way, round-trip, and nonstop charter flights across the Taiwan Strait starting in February 2005. This development was dampened by Taiwan's reactions to legislation adopted by China's National People's Congress (NPC) on March 14, 2005, "for the purpose of opposing and checking Taiwan's secession from China by secessionists in the name of "Taiwan independence." However, soon thereafter, further developments occurred that Beijing found more favorable to Taiwan reunification. These occurred when the leaders of three Taiwan political parties made separate trips to China between March and May 2005. First, Kuomintang Vice Chairman Chiang Pin-kung led a delegation to China to initiate talks on cross-strait economics and trade. Then the chairman of the Kuomintang, Lien Chan, made a "journey of peace" visit and signed a joint communiqué with CCP General Secretary Hu Jintao concerning the promotion of cross-strait exchanges and cooperation. Finally, James Soong, chairman of the People First Party, visited China. All three trips were strictly party-to-party meetings. These visits to the mainland were followed by a delegation of the New Party led by its chairman, Mok Mu-ming in July 2005.

Judicial and Legal System: In 2004 the National People's Congress (NPC) amended the constitution so that for the first time the protection of the individual was incorporated as a constitutional requirement. Specifically, Articles 37 and 38 recognize the "freedom of the person" and the "personal dignity of citizens" as "inviolable." Although the 1997 Criminal Procedure Law allows the police to detain a person for up to 37 days before release or formal arrest, more vigorous court reviews have led to the release of thousands of unlawfully detained individuals. However, although the law stipulates that the authorities must notify a detainee's family or work unit of the detention within 24 hours, in practice timely notification is often disregarded, especially in sensitive political cases. Police sometimes hold individuals without granting access to family members or lawyers, and their trials are sometimes conducted in secret. Detained criminal suspects, defendants, their legal representatives, and close relatives are entitled to apply for bail, but, in practice, few suspects are released pending trial. The reeducation-through-labor system allows nonjudicial panels of police and local civil authorities to sentence individuals to up to three years in prison-like facilities. It has been reported that some detainees, usually political activists or dissidents, have been incarcerated in high-security psychiatric facilities for the criminally insane. Police and prosecutorial officials have been accused of ignoring due process provisions of the law and constitution.

Citizens have a constitutional guarantee of the right to use their own spoken and written language in court proceedings. Courts and procuratorates are advised by the constitution that they "should provide translations for any party to the court proceedings who is not familiar with the spoken or written languages in common use in the locality." The constitution provides for an independent judiciary, but the courts are subjected to party and government policy guidance that influences the outcome of verdicts and sentences. Conviction rates in criminal cases in the early 2000s were approximately 90 percent, and trials generally were little more than sentencing hearings. Although most suspects in criminal cases are legally guaranteed the right to counsel, they often meet their appointed attorney only once before the hearing; at best, a defense attorney can obtain a reduction of the sentence. In many politically sensitive trials, rarely lasting more than several hours, the courts hand down guilty verdicts immediately following proceedings, and death sentences are often implemented within days of the rejection of an appeal.

Electoral System: Under the Organic Law of the Village Committees, all of China's approximately 1 million villages are expected to hold competitive, direct elections for subgovernmental village committees. A 1998 revision to the law called for improvements in the nominating process and enhanced transparency in village committee administration. The revised law also explicitly transferred the power to nominate candidates to villagers themselves, as opposed to village groups or Chinese Communist Party (CCP) branches. According to the Ministry of Civil Affairs, as of 2003 the majority of provinces had carried out at least four or five rounds of village elections. Deputies to local people's congresses of provinces, centrally administered municipalities, and cities divided into districts are elected by the people's congress at the next lower level. Deputies to people's congresses of counties, cities not divided into districts, municipal districts, townships, ethnic townships, and towns are elected directly by their constituencies to five-year terms. The local congresses each have corresponding standing committees that exercise legislative authority when the full congresses are not in session. Some townships and urban areas also have experimented with direct elections of local government leaders, plus local people's congresses have the constitutional authority to recall the heads and deputy heads of government at the provincial level and below. The constitution does not specify how deputies to the people's congresses of the autonomous regions, autonomous prefectures, and autonomous counties are chosen. Elected leaders, however, remain subordinate to the corresponding CCP secretary, and most are appointed by higher-level party organizations. Although China's constitution guarantees suffrage for citizens age 18 and older, the CCP maintains a close watch on electoral democracy at the grassroots levels and controls the outcome of elections at other levels.

Politics and Political Parties: After its founding in July 1921, the Chinese Communist Party (CCP) had only 57 members and little influence, but by 2005 the CCP had 70.8 million members and controlled all political, governmental, and military organs. Although political reform was not one of the Four Modernizations promulgated so earnestly after 1978, the CCP has allowed greater participation by nonparty members in economic and social developments. Within the party, the CCP practices what it calls "democratic centralism," which, in effect, means that the minority follows the decisions of the majority, each level follows the directives of the next highest level, and all follow the lead of the party's center. Constitutionally, the CCP's national congress is the party's highest body. It is convened every five years, usually prior to the National People's Congress. However, to operate, it elects a Central Committee, which in turn elects (or approves) the members of the Political Bureau and that organ's even more elite Standing Committee. The current Central Committee has 198 members and 158 alternate members. The Political Bureau has 24 members and one alternate member, and its Standing Committee has nine members, including Hu Jintao, who became CCP general secretary in November 2002, succeeding Jiang Zemin. Of its 66.4 million members, 16.6 percent are women, only 6.1 percent members of minority nationalities, and 23.1 percent under age 35. Unlike the largely peasant, worker, and military veteran party of the past, 29.2 percent are high-school graduates, 17.8 percent of CCP members have undergraduate degrees, and 0.5 percent have graduate degrees.

When Mao led the party from 1935 to his death in 1976, he held the position of CCP chairman. His immediate and short-term successor Hua Guofeng also held the title of chairman, as did Hua's successor when he took office in 1981, Hu Yaobang, who held the title for a short time until the position was then abolished at the CCP Twelfth Party Congress in September 1982, endowing the general secretary as the most powerful position in the party. Deng Xiaoping, despite being the paramount leader in China in the post-Mao era, never held the top party or state positions. Instead, he allowed more junior leaders to hold these positions. When Deng's longest-term successor, Jiang Zemin, retired in stages between 2002 and 2004, he appeared to have assumed a similar behind-the-throne position of influence.

Day-to-day management of the CCP is carried out by a central secretariat and various functional departments: the International Liaison Department, United Front Work Department, Organization Department, Propaganda Department, and Party Central Academy. Party secretaries are found at all levels of government and the military and in industries, academia, and other parts of society. In 2004 the CCP reported more than 3.3 million party branches throughout the nation. Its main organs are the daily newspaper *Renmin Ribao* (People's Daily) and the semimonthly theoretical journal *Qiu Shi* (Seeking Truth, formerly titled *Hongqi*, or Red Flag).

China also has titular "democratic" parties that were loyal to the CCP in the pre-1949 period and continue to function within the structure of the Chinese People's Political Consultative Conference (CPPCC), namely, the China Association for Promoting Democracy, China Democratic League, China Democratic National Construction Association, China Zhigongdang (Party for Public Interest), Chinese Peasants' and Workers' Democratic Party, Jiusan (September Third—a reference to the date of the defeat of Japan in 1945) Society, Guomindang Revolutionary Committee, and Taiwan Self-Government League. An independent opposition party, the China Democracy Party, has been banned since 1998 and its leaders arrested.

Mass Media: China's electronic mass media are regulated by the State Administration of Radio, Film, and Television, a subordinate agency of the Ministry of Information Industry. The Chinese Communist Party's Propaganda Department traditionally has played a large role as arbiter of standards for appropriate broadcasts. The People's Broadcasting Station transmits radio broadcasts in standard Chinese (Putonghua) and the various dialects and minority languages throughout China. In 2004, 282 domestic radio stations and 774 short- and medium-wave radio relaying and transmitting stations operated, and many stations provided Internet access to some of their broadcasts. China National Radio, headquartered in Beijing, transmits programs in standard Chinese, Kazakh, Korean, Mongolian, Tibetan, and Uygur. China Radio International, also headquartered in Beijing but with domestic service branches in major cities, broadcasts in 43 foreign languages and several Chinese dialects. Television service is provided by China Central Television (CCTV) in Beijing along with extensive local daily programming and Internet access by viewers to scheduling, reviews, and programming. By 2001 CCTV had 33 local affiliates, along provincial lines, with areas such as Fujian and Shanghai having two stations. China Education Television (CETV) also is used for distance learning. Cable television was reaching 114.7 million households, or about 95 percent of the population, by the end of 2004.

The government has been active in regulating newspapers in the twenty-first century. Although foreign investment in local news media was permissible by 2002, the government closed down 673 unprofitable state-run newspapers in 2003 and in 2004 banned subscription newspapers and periodicals. The major national newspaper, *Renmin Ribao* (People's Daily), was established in 1948 as the main organ of the Chinese Communist Party, has a print circulation of nearly 2.2 million, and offers overseas editions and Internet access in foreign languages. Other major newspapers published in Beijing are *Gongren Ribao* (Workers' Daily), *Nongmin Ribao* (Farmers' Daily), *Zhongguo Qingnian Bao* (China Youth News), *Guangming Ribao* (Bright

Daily), *Jiefangjun Bao* (Liberation Army Daily), and *Zhongguo Ribao* (China Daily). There are two major newspapers published outside of Beijing: *Jiefang Ribao* (Liberation Daily), published in Shanghai, and *Nanfang Ribao* (Southern Daily), published in Guangzhou. These newspapers have circulations of between 300,000 and 2.5 million and also include Internet editions. China had more than 2,000 other newspapers in publication in 2006.

China published 208, 294 books, with a total print run of 6.4 million volumes, in 2004 and printed 2,119 newspapers with a total average circulation of 190.7 million in 2003. Even more widely distributed were China's 9,074 magazines, which in 2003 rose to an average circulation of 199 million copies and probably more since both newspapers and magazines typically are traded among multiple readers, and newspapers often are posted on community bulletin boards for passers-by.

The Ministry of Information Industry regulates access to the Internet while the Ministry of Public Security and the Ministry of State Security monitor its use. A broad range of topics that authorities interpret as potentially subversive or as slanderous to the state, including the dissemination of anti-unification information or "state secrets" that may endanger national security, are prohibited by various laws and regulations. Promoting "evil cults" (a term used for Falun Gong) is banned, as is providing information that "disturbs social order or undermines social stability." Internet service providers (ISPs) are restricted to domestic media news postings and are required to record information useful for tracking users and their viewing habits, install software capable of copying e-mails, and immediately abort transmission of material considered subversive. As a result, many ISPs practice self-censorship to avoid violations of the broadly worded regulations.

Foreign Relations: At a national meeting on diplomatic work in August 2004, China's president Hu Jintao reiterated that China will continue its "independent foreign policy of peaceful development," stressing the need for a peaceful and stable international environment, especially among China's neighbors, that will foster "mutually beneficial cooperation" and "common development." This policy line has varied little in intent since the People's Republic was established in 1949, but the rhetoric has varied in its stridency to reflect periods of domestic political upheaval.

At its inception, the People's Republic had a close relationship with the Soviet Union and the Eastern Bloc nations, sealed with, among other agreements, the China-Soviet Treaty of Friendship, Alliance, and Mutual Assistance signed in 1950 to oppose China's chief antagonists, the West and in particular the United States. The 1950–53 Korean War waged by China and its North Korea ally against the United States, South Korea, and United Nations (UN) forces has long been a reason for bitter feelings. By the late 1950s, relations between China and the Soviet Union had become so divisive that in 1960 the Soviets unilaterally withdrew their advisers from China. The two then began to vie for allegiances among the developing world nations, for China saw itself as a natural champion through its role in the Non-Aligned Movement and its numerous bilateral and bi-party ties. By 1969 relations with Moscow were so tense that fighting erupted along their common border. China then lessened its anti-Western rhetoric and began developing formal diplomatic relations with West European nations.

Around the same time, in 1971, that Beijing succeeded in gaining China's seat in the UN (thus ousting the Republic of China on Taiwan), relations with the United States began to thaw. In 1973 President Richard M. Nixon visited China. Formal diplomatic relations were established in 1978, and the two nations have experienced more than a quarter century of varying degrees of amiable or wary relations over such contentious issues as Taiwan, trade balances, intellectual property rights, nuclear proliferation, and human rights. In October 2005, Secretary of Defense Donald Rumsfeld visited Beijing at the invitation of the minister of national defense and vice chairman of the Central Military Commission, Cao Gangchuan. Cao and Rumsfeld exchanged views on regional and international issues as well as on the future development of bilateral relations between their nations and armed forces. They agreed to work toward placing military relations on a level "commensurate with the relations with the two countries"

China's relations with its Asian neighbors have become stable during the last decades of the twentieth century. Despite a border war with India in 1962 and general distrust between the two (mostly over China's close relationship with Pakistan and India's with the former Soviet Union), in the early 2000s relations between the world's two largest nations have never been more harmonious. China had long been a close ally of North Korea but also found a valuable trading partner in South Korea and eventually took a role in the early 2000s as a proponent of "six-party talks" (North Korea, South Korea, Russia, Japan, the United States, and China) to resolve tensions on the Korean Peninsula. On November 15, 2005, Hu Jintao visited Seoul and spoke of the importance of both countries' contributions for regional peace and cooperation in economic development. Japan, with its large economic and cultural influences in Asia, is seen by China as its most formidable opponent and partner in regional diplomacy. The two sides established diplomatic relations in 1972, and Japanese investment in China was important in the early years of China's economic reforms and ever since. Having fought two wars against Japan (1894–95 and 1936–45), China's long-standing concern about the level of Japan's military strength surfaces periodically, and criticism of Japan's refusal to present a full version of the atrocities of World War II in its textbooks is a perennial issue. China has stable relations with its neighbors to the south. A border war was fought with one-time close ally Vietnam in 1979, but relations have improved since then. A territorial dispute with its Southeast Asian neighbors over islands in the South China Sea remains unresolved, as does another dispute in the East China Sea with Japan.

The end of the long-held animosity between Moscow and Beijing was marked by the visit to China by Soviet President Mikhail Gorbachev in 1989. After the 1991 demise of the Soviet Union, China's relations with the Russian Federation and the former states of the Soviet Union became more amicable. A new round of bilateral agreements was signed during reciprocal head of state visits. As in the early 1950s with the Soviet Union, Russia has again become an important source of military matériel for China, as well as for raw materials and trade. Friendly relations with Russia have been an important advantage for China, offsetting its often uneasy relations with the United States. Relations with Europe, both Eastern and Western, generally have been friendly in the early twenty-first century, and, indeed, close political and trade relations with the European Union nations have been a major thrust of China's foreign policy in the 2000s. In November 2005, President Hu Jintao visited the United Kingdom, Germany, and Spain and announced China's eagerness to enter into greater political and economic cooperation with its European partners.

Although committed to good relations with the nations of the Middle East, Africa, and Latin America, in the twenty-first century China finds perhaps the greatest value in these areas as markets and sources of raw materials. The years of solidarity with revolutionary movements in these regions have long been replaced by efforts to cultivate normal diplomatic and economic relations.

Membership in International Organizations: China holds a permanent seat, which affords it veto power, on the Security Council of the United Nations (UN). Prior to 1971, the Republic of China on Taiwan held China's UN seat, but, as of that date, the People's Republic of China successfully lobbied for Taiwan's removal from the UN and took control of the seat. China is an active member of numerous UN system organizations, including the UN General Assembly and Security Council; Food and Agriculture Organization of the UN; UN Conference on Trade and Development; UN Educational, Scientific and Cultural Organization; UN Office of the High Commissioner for Refugees; UN Industrial Development Organization; UN Institute for Training and Research; UN Monitoring, Verification, and Inspection Commission; and UN Truce Supervision Organization. China also holds memberships in the African Development Bank, Asian Development Bank, Asia Pacific Economic Cooperation, Association of Southeast Asian Nations (dialogue partner), Association of Southeast Asian Nations Regional Forum, Bank for International Settlements, Caribbean Development Bank, Group of 77, International Atomic Energy Agency, International Bank for Reconstruction and Development, International Chamber of Commerce, International Civil Aviation Organization, International Criminal Police Organization, International Development Association, International Federation of Red Cross and Red Crescent Societies, International Finance Corporation, International Fund for Agricultural Development, International Hydrographic Organization, International Labour Organization, International Maritime Organization, International Monetary Fund, International Olympic Committee, International Organization for Migration (observer), International Organization for Standardization, International Red Cross and Red Crescent Movement, International Telecommunication Union, Latin American Integration Association (observer), Non-Aligned Movement (observer), Organisation for the Prohibition of Chemical Weapons, Permanent Court of Arbitration, Shanghai Cooperation Organization, Universal Postal Union, World Customs Organization, World Health Organization, World Intellectual Property Organization, World Meteorological Organization, World Tourism Organization, World Trade Organization, and Zangger Committee.

Major International Treaties: The People's Republic of China has signed numerous international conventions and treaties. Treaties signed on behalf of China before 1949 are applicable only to the Republic of China on Taiwan. Conventions signed by Beijing include: Assistance in Case of a Nuclear Accident or Radiological Emergency Convention; Biological and Toxin Weapons Convention; Chemical Weapons Convention; Conventional Weapons Convention; Early Notification of a Nuclear Accident Convention; Inhumane Weapons Convention; Nuclear Dumping Convention (London Convention); Nuclear Safety Convention; Physical Protection of Nuclear Material Convention; Rights of the Child and on the Sale of Children, Child Prostitution, and Child Pornography Convention (signed Optional Protocol); and Status of Refugees (and the 1967 Protocol) Convention. Treaties include the Comprehensive Test Ban Treaty (signed but not ratified); Protocol for the Prohibition of the Use in War of Asphyxiating, Poisonous, or Other Gases, and of Bacteriological Methods of Warfare (Geneva

Protocol); Treaty on the African Nuclear-Weapon-Free Zone (Treaty of Pelindaba, signed protocols 1 and 2); Treaty on the Non-Proliferation of Nuclear Weapons; Treaty on Outer Space; Treaty for the Prohibition of Nuclear Weapons in Latin America and the Caribbean (Treaty of Tlatelolco, signed Protocol 2); Treaty on Seabed Arms Control; and Treaty on the South Pacific Nuclear-Free Zone (Treaty of Rarotonga, signed and ratified protocols 2 and 3). China also is a party to the following international environmental conventions: Antarctic-Environmental Protocol, Antarctic Treaty, Biodiversity, Climate Change, Climate Change-Kyoto Protocol, Desertification, Endangered Species, Hazardous Wastes, Law of the Sea, Marine Dumping, Ozone Layer Protection, Ship Pollution, Tropical Timber 83, Tropical Timber 94, Wetlands, and Whaling.

NATIONAL SECURITY

Armed Forces Overview: The armed forces of China are officially and collectively known as the People's Liberation Army (PLA). The ground forces are referred to simply as the PLA, but the navy is called the PLA Navy and the air force is known as the PLA Air Force. The PLA's independent strategic missile forces are often referred to as the PLA Second Artillery Corps. The Chinese Communist Party (CCP) Central Military Commission sets policy for the PLA. The commission, which is chaired by China's president, has three vice chairmen, each a general in the PLA ground forces, and seven members representing various components of the PLA. Operational control is administered dually by the CCP Central Military Commission and the State Central Military Commission and the Ministry of National Defense. PLA headquarters is organized into the General Staff Department, General Political Department, General Logistics Department, and General Armaments Department. In 2005 China announced that it downsized its military by 200,000 troops in order to optimize force structures and increase combat capabilities. The active-duty troop numbers declined to 2.3 million, compared to 3.2 million in 1987. The changes included eliminating layers in the command hierarchy, reducing noncombat units, such as schools and farms, and reprogramming officer duties. The number of ground forces was reduced by the largest margin, while the navy, air force, and Second Artillery Corps were strengthened. An estimated 1.7 million military personnel are in the ground forces, 250,000 in the navy (including 26,000 naval aviation, 10,000 marines, and 28,000 coastal defense forces), an estimated 400,000 to 420,000 in the air force, and 90,000–100,000 in the strategic missile forces. Reservists number an estimated 500,000 to 600,000 and paramilitary forces in the People's Armed Police an estimated 1.5 million.

The Central Military Commission of the People's Republic of China is constitutionally different from the Central Military Commission of the Chinese Communist Party. According to Article 93 of the state constitution, the state Central Military Commission directs the armed forces of the country and is composed of a chairman (currently Hu Jintao since June 2004), vice chairmen, and members whose terms run concurrently with the National People's Congress. The commission is responsible to the NPC and its Standing Committee.

Foreign Military Relations: China sold US$800 million worth of arms and military equipment to a variety of nations in 2002, making it the world's fifth largest arms supplier after the United States, United Kingdom, Russia, and France. Among its principal clients have been Algeria,

Egypt, Iran, Kuwait, Pakistan, and Yemen. China also provides military assistance to other countries, such as Fiji, Papua New Guinea, Tonga, and Vanuatu. The China North Industries Group Corporation (CNGC, often called NORINCO), China's main defense producer, has some 100 joint ventures and more than 80 overseas offices and branches in 30 countries and regions involved in military and dual-use technology production and sales. Further, China is also a major arms buyer, mostly naval and air force equipment from Russia. In 2004 China gave unprecedented access to senior foreign military officers at a military demonstration in Henan Province. Officers from 15 Asian nations and Russia were present. In 2005 China and Russia held joint eight-day "Peace Mission 2005" military maneuvers near Vladisvostok and in Shandong Province and nearby waters. Air, land, and amphibious exercises were held.

China is a member of the Shanghai Cooperation Organization (SCO), a joint effort with Russia, Kazakhstan, Kyrgyzstan, Tajikistan, and Uzbekistan. The SCO was established as the Shanghai Five when the partners signed agreements on strengthening mutual trust in military fields in border areas in 1996 and on mutual reduction of military forces in border areas in 1997. After the September 11, 2001, terrorist attacks on the United States and the entry of U.S. and North Atlantic Treaty Organization (NATO) forces into Central Asia, the SCO was formed and members began to hold joint counterterrorism military exercises. In 2004 the SCO initiated a regional antiterrorism structure to crack down on various transnational terrorist and criminal activities. China also has held joint naval and counterterrorism exercises with Pakistan. The naval exercise, which occurred in the East China Sea, was the first such drill with a foreign counterpart, as Chinese sources put it, "in a non-traditional security field." The antiterrorism exercise, which was held in Xinjiang Uygur Autonomous Region, involved border guards from both sides.

External Threat: Even while embroiled in the problems of territorial disputes with its neighbors and the dangers of periodic tensions on the Korean Peninsula and across the Taiwan Strait, China perceives the United States as its major threat. Beijing believes that the United States still maintains its Cold War policy toward China and the Asia-Pacific region and stresses ideological differences and their relationship to security issues of concern in the region. In China's view, Washington's attitude exacerbates tensions, which, in turn, lead to international turmoil. Post-Soviet Russia is now fairly benign in China's view, and relations have improved significantly from the days of border conflicts and high-level tension. Concerns about the remilitarization of Japan also resurface on occasion, often as a legacy of World War II enmity. Transnational crime, terrorism, separatism, and contradictions among nations all contribute to China's security concerns.

Defense Budget: Although China claims that the share of defense spending as a percentage of the overall state budget has declined from 17.4 percent in 1979 to 9.5 percent in 1994 and 7.7 percent in 2004, the government has announced double-digit increases in military spending nearly every year for more than a decade. The defense budget for 2006 is expected to reach US$35.1 billion, the largest increase in four years and 16 percent higher than 2005 (estimated at US$29.5 billion). The report submitted in March 2006 at the Fourth Session of the 10th National People's Congress (NPC) contained a request for a budget increase to strengthen China's defensive capability and ability to respond to emergencies and to raise officer and enlisted pay levels. The NPC stated that China's military spending is still low compared to the United States,

United Kingdom, France, Germany, and Japan. However, the actual defense budget is likely to be higher than expected because of the inclusion of defense-related items in nondefense budgets.

Major Military Units: The ground forces are organized into seven military regions (headquartered in Shenyang in the northeast, Beijing in the north, Lanzhou in the west, Chengdu in the southwest, Guangzhou in the south, Jinan in central China, and Nanjing in the east), 28 provincial military districts, four centrally controlled garrison commands (coinciding with the centrally administered municipalities of Beijing, Tianjin, Shanghai, and Chongqing), and 21 integrated group armies. The group armies have strengths between 30,000 and 65,000 troops. Each group army typically has two or three infantry divisions, one armored division or brigade, one artillery division or brigade, and one joint surface-to-air missile or antiaircraft artillery brigade or simply an antiaircraft artillery brigade.

The navy is organized into North Sea (headquartered at Qingdao, Shandong Province), East Sea (headquartered at Ningbo, Zhejiang Province), and South Sea (headquartered at Zhanjiang, Guangdong Province) fleets. Each fleet has destroyer, submarine, and coastal patrol flotillas, possibly even amphibious flotillas, and naval air stations. There are numerous major naval bases: the North Sea Fleet has seven, the East Sea Fleet eight, and the South Sea Fleet 16.

The air force has five air corps and 32 air divisions. The major air force headquarters coincide with the seven military regions. The air force has more than 140 air bases and airfields, including ready access to China's major regional and international airports.

The strategic missile forces, or Second Artillery Corps, are organized into seven missile divisions based in the military regions, with the central headquarters at Qinghe, north of Beijing. There also are training and testing bases. The six operational bases had some 21 launch brigades in 2005.

Major Military Equipment: The major ground forces equipment includes an estimated 7,000 main battle tanks, 1,200 light tanks, 5,000 armored personnel carriers, 14,000 pieces of towed artillery, 1,700 pieces of self-propelled artillery, 2,400 multiple-rocket launchers, 7,700 air defense guns, 6,500 antitank guided weapons, and unspecified numbers of mortars, surface-to-surface and surface-to-air missiles, recoilless rifles, rocket launchers, and antitank guns. The ground forces also have an estimated 321 helicopters and an unspecified number of unmanned air vehicles and surveillance aircraft.

Among its principal combatant ships, the navy has 68 submarines (many of which are slated for decommissioning in the mid-2000s). One is a Xia class submarine-launched ballistic missile (SSBN) force strategic-capability submarine. There are plans for more advanced SSBNs by the end of the decade. The navy also has an estimated 21 destroyers and 42 frigates, as well as 368 fast-attack craft, 39 mine warfare ships, 10 hovercraft, 6 troop transports, 19 landing-ship/tank ships, 37 medium landing ships, 45 utility landing craft, 10 air-cushioned landing craft, 163 support and miscellaneous craft, 8 submarine support ships, 4 salvage and repair ships, 29 supply ships, 1 multirole aviation ship, and about 700 land-based combat aircraft and 45 armed helicopters. China also has plans to launch a 40,000-ton aircraft carrier by 2010.

The air force has some 1,900 combat aircraft, including armed helicopters. The inventory includes 180 bombers, more than 950 fighters and 838 ground attack fighters, an estimated 290 reconnaissance/electronic intelligence aircraft, an estimated 513 transports, an estimated 170 helicopters, some 200 training aircraft, and an unmanned aerial vehicle. Weapons include air-to-air missiles and ground-based air defense artillery using surface-to-air missiles and antiaircraft artillery.

The strategic missile forces have in their inventory 20 or more intercontinental ballistic missiles (ICBMs), between 130 and 150 intermediate-range ballistic missiles, one Xia class submarine carrying 12 submarine-launched ballistic missiles, and about 335 or more short-range ballistic missiles.

Military Service: There is selective conscription of two years for all the services starting at age 18 for males. In 2004 there were some 136,000 women in the armed forces.

Paramilitary Forces: The principal paramilitary organization is the People's Armed Police Force. There are militia forces of indeterminate strength under the control of the Chinese Communist Party (CCP). Once a critical part of Mao Zedong's "people's war" strategy, militia units are no longer an essential part of China's military and have mostly disbanded.

Military Forces Abroad: In 2004 China deployed 95 riot police officers as part of a 125-member unit to Haiti for the United Nations (UN) Stabilization Mission in Haiti, a nation with which Beijing does not have diplomatic relations. As of that time, China had deployed 297 peacekeepers to five other nations, including East Timor, Bosnia-Herzegovina, Liberia, Afghanistan, and the autonomous province of Kosovo in Serbia and Montenegro. China also has sent peacekeeping observers to Ethiopia and Eritrea, various Middle Eastern countries, the Democratic Republic of the Congo, Sierra Leone, and Western Sahara. It is a formal participant in the UN Mission for the Referendum in Western Sahara, UN Organization Mission in the Democratic Republic of the Congo, UN Mission in Sierra Leone, UN Mission in Ethiopia and Eritrea, and UN Mission in Liberia.

Police and Internal Security: The security apparatus is made up of the Ministry of State Security and the Ministry of Public Security, the People's Armed Police, the People's Liberation Army (PLA), and the state judicial, procuratorial, and penal systems. The Ministry of Public Security oversees all domestic police activity in China, including the People's Armed Police Force. The ministry is responsible for police operations and prisons and has dedicated departments for internal political, economic, and communications security. Its lowest organizational units are public security stations, which maintain close day-to-day contact with the public. The People's Armed Police Force, which sustains an estimated total strength of 1.5 million personnel, is organized into 45 divisions: internal security police, border defense personnel, guards for government buildings and embassies, and police communications specialists.

The Ministry of State Security was established in 1983 to ensure "the security of the state through effective measures against enemy agents, spies, and counterrevolutionary activities designed to sabotage or overthrow China's socialist system." The ministry is guided by a series of laws enacted in 1993, 1994, and 1997 that replaced the "counterrevolutionary" crime statutes. The ministry's operations include intelligence collection, both domestic and foreign. Authorities have used arrests on charges of revealing state secrets, subversion, and common crimes to suppress political dissent and social advocacy.

Internal Threat and Terrorism: Although the government defines the outlawed Falun Gong movement as the major internal threat and the People's Armed Police Force actively pursues its members, Falun Gong is, nevertheless, not classified as a terrorist group, and it has not committed or sponsored acts of violence. Muslim separatists in Xinjiang Uygur Autonomous Region present China with its most significant terrorist threat, which emerged in the late 1980s. In 2003 Beijing published an "East Turkistan Terrorist List," which labeled organizations such as the World Uighur Youth Congress and the East Turkistan Information Center as terrorist entities. These groups openly advocate independence for "East Turkestan," and, although they have not been publicly linked to violent activity, the separatists have resorted to violence, bomb attacks, assassinations, and street fighting, which Beijing responds to with police and military action. During the summer of 2004, elite troops from China and Pakistan held joint antiterrorism exercises in Xinjiang that were aimed at the East Turkistan Islamic Movement, an organization listed as terrorist by China, the United States, and the United Nations (UN). This and other Uygur separatist groups reputedly were trained in Afghanistan to fight with the Taliban and al Qaeda. The East Turkistan Islamic Movement was established in 1990 and has links to the Islamic Movement of Uzbekistan, which operates throughout Central Asia. Premier Wen Jiabao joined leaders of other Asian and European nations in Hanoi for the October 2004 Asia-Europe Meeting (ASEM) in Hanoi, where the delegates reaffirmed their call for a war on terrorism led by the UN.

Human Rights: Article 34 of China's constitution states that the "state respects and guarantees human rights" and that "every citizen is entitled to the rights and at the same time must perform the duties prescribed by the constitution and the law." The following article guarantees "freedom of speech, of the press, of assembly, of association, of procession and of demonstration." Compared to the earlier years of stringent rule by the Maoist regime, China's citizens enjoy a much wider range of human rights and basic exercise of their constitutional freedoms. Although tightly regulated, the mass media are relatively more freewheeling than in the past. Economic reforms have brought a new measure of individual expression and great wealth and influence for some. Police reports from China indicate that the number and size of public protests have multiplied rapidly since the early 1990s and that such protests are now counted in the tens of thousands. For example, police recorded 32,000 protests in 1999 alone. According to later official statistics, however, "public order disturbances" were much lower, reportedly only 87 during 2005, a 6.6 percent increase from 2004. However, the Ministry of Public Security claimed that incidents described as mob violence also rose by 13 percent over 2004, and the number of demonstrations continued to grow as protesters became more organized during the year.

However, citizens cannot express opposition to the Chinese Communist Party (CCP)-led political system and do not have the right to change their national leaders or form of government. Socialism is still the theoretical basis of national politics and although Marxist economic planning gave way to pragmatism, economic decentralization has merely increased the authority of local officials. The party's authority rests primarily on the government's ability to maintain social stability through appeals to nationalism and patriotism; party control of personnel, media, and the security apparatus; and continued improvement of living standards. Although the constitution provides for an independent judiciary, in practice the government and the CCP, at both the central and local levels, frequently intercede in the judicial process and direct verdicts in many high-profile cases. While the number of religious believers in China continues to increase, governmental respect for religious freedom has remained poor. The government, which regulates, manages, and controls the broadcast media, has censored foreign broadcasts, at times jamming radio signals from abroad. In 2003 some publications were closed and otherwise disciplined for publishing material deemed objectionable by the government, and journalists, authors, academics, and researchers were reportedly harassed, detained, and arrested by the authorities.

Under party guidance, civilian authorities generally maintain effective control of the security forces, but according to data provided by the U.S. Department of State, security personnel are responsible for numerous human rights abuses. Despite the growing number of protests that have occurred in China and continued legal reforms, in 2003 arrests continually took place of individuals discussing sensitive subjects on the Internet and of health activists, labor protesters, defense lawyers, journalists, underground church members, and others seeking to take advantage of the government-fostered reforms. Abuses of the judicial system included instances of extrajudicial killings, torture and mistreatment of prisoners, forced confessions, arbitrary arrest and detention, lengthy incommunicado detention, and denial of due process. In the same year, more than 250,000 persons were incarcerated in "reeducation-through-labor" camps under sentences not subject to judicial review. Moreover, some 500 to 600 individuals were serving out sentences for the now-repealed crime of counterrevolution, and an estimated 2,000 persons remained in prison in 2003 for their activities during the June 1989 Tiananmen demonstrations, which were violently suppressed by the People's Liberation Army (PLA). China has active human rights dialogues with numerous countries, including Australia, Canada, Chile, Germany, Japan, the United Kingdom, and the United States, as well as with the European Union.

The U.S. Department of State also reported several positive human rights developments during 2005. The government returned authority to approve death sentences to the Supreme People's Court, supported local experiments to record police interrogation of suspects, and limited the administrative detention of minors, the elderly, pregnant women, and nursing mothers. In March 2005, government officials stated that family bible studies in private homes need not be registered with the government and permitted the religious education of minors. However, problems continued in both areas. The National People's Congress adopted amendments to the law protecting woman's rights and interests, including one outlawing sexual harassment. The government ratified International Labour Organization Convention 111 prohibiting discrimination in employment and also hosted visits by international human rights monitors.

www.ingramcontent.com/pod-product-compliance
Lightning Source LLC
Chambersburg PA
CBHW080628290526
45790CB00007B/2977